FRANCIS THOMPSON
AND
WILFRID MEYNELL

D1093917

FRANCIS THOMPSON
about 1894

Francis
THOMPSON
and
Wilfrid
MEYNELL

A memoir by

VIOLA MEYNELL

EST·1852

New York

E. P. DUTTON & CO., INC.

1953

Copyright, 1952, by E. P. Dutton & Co., Inc.
All rights reserved. Printed in the U.S.A.

FIRST EDITION

No part of this book may be reproduced
in any form without permission in writing
from the publisher, except by a reviewer
who wishes to quote brief passages in con-
nection with a review written for inclusion in
magazine or newspaper or radio broadcast.

Library of Congress Catalog Card No. 52-12333

DEDICATED TO SEBASTIAN MEYNELL

NOTE

THE sources from which the contents of this book are drawn are chiefly letters preserved by Wilfrid Meynell of which few have hitherto been published. No other account of Wilfrid Meynell has been written. The *Life of Francis Thompson* by Everard Meynell has related Thompson's story, and letters contained in it are here repeated and supplemented. Wilfrid Blunt's *My Diaries* has been drawn upon. Memory supplies much else.

LIST OF ILLUSTRATIONS

FRANCIS THOMPSON, from a photograph by Francis
Bacon, 1894 (*by courtesy of Thomas Nelson & Sons*)   *frontispiece*

WILFRID MEYNELL, as a young man . . . . *facing page* 56

ALICE MEYNELL, about the time of her marriage . "   "   57

HENRY EDWARD CARDINAL MANNING,
from the engraving by Mortimer Menpes . . . "   "   64

WILFRID SCAWEN BLUNT, about 1900 . . . "   "   65

KATIE KING . . . . "   "   116

COVENTRY PATMORE . . . . "   "   117

WILFRID MEYNELL, in middle age . . . . . . "   "   132

AUTOGRAPH LETTER from Francis Thompson to
Wilfrid Meynell . . . . "   "   133

FRANCIS THOMPSON, from the painting by
Everard Meynell, about 1906 . . . . "   "   180

EVERARD MEYNELL, from a photograph by
Sherril Schell . . . . "   "   181

ALICE MEYNELL, in late life, from a photograph
by E. O. Hoppé . . . . "   "   196

WILFRID MEYNELL, from a portrait by Olivia
Sowerby in 1936 . . . . "   "   197

FRANCIS THOMPSON
AND
WILFRID MEYNELL

I

THIS is the story of the association of two men. They met strangely, lived differently, and were peculiarly and fatefully united. As one of them was a poet, Francis Thompson, and one a journalist, Wilfrid Meynell, it might be thought that this account should make some estimate of their achievements and place in their respective worlds. But that is outside the knowledge or ability of one whose only attempt is to give the personal story and characteristics of the two of them; in fact if ever a book were open to the charge of "indulging in personalities" it should be this one, with that for its only object. It will digress into their relations with others, to suggest the surrounding of their association of nineteen years: and it will be compiled with the aid of the collections of letters stowed away in a Sussex library, many of them untouched for three-quarters of a century.

Wilfrid Meynell was born at Picton House in Newcastle-on-Tyne in 1852, the seventh child of a small colliery owner. His mother was one of the Tukes of York, who were initiators of humane treatment of the insane—till then chained and fettered. It was in 1792 that William Tuke proposed the providing of a "Retired Habitation for those who may be in a state of lunacy"— afterwards known as the Retreat. The Meynells, like the Tukes, were Quakers, and the sons went to Bootham School in York. As a boy Wilfrid, who had temporary thoughts of a chemistry career, was impressed by an encounter he had with Sir James Simpson, the inventor of chloroform. Simpson's biographer records how on one of his journeys between London and Edinburgh Simpson "stopped at York, dined at Lord Houghton's, and went to chat with a medical friend till the night mail picked him up." The medical friend, Wilfrid Meynell wrote later, "was my

Uncle, Dr. Caleb Williams, a brother *soul*. I must have been about 14 or 15 when Simpson asked me to kneel down with him, and offered prayers that I might follow in his footsteps as a *Healer*. When we rose from our knees he put his arm on my shoulder and said: 'Pain, my boy, I have made it an oblivion: it is for you to make it an ecstasy.' "

Though his brothers were at Bootham School for much longer, Wilfrid had only one year there, from the age of fifteen to sixteen, after being at the—also Quaker—Ackworth School at Croydon. Gaps in the education of a boy not interested in education were never filled up. It was religion and poetry that drew him in his teens, and at the age of eighteen he left the Society of Friends for the Roman Catholic Church, being received into it by Father Antoninus Williams, O.P., of Newcastle. This was the final outcome of a chance encounter with Father Antoninus in a train between London and Newcastle. In that leisurely journey a sensitive youth had the good fortune to meet with a sweet and generous temperament, of which a glimpse is shown in a letter written by Father Antoninus some years later when Wilfrid Meynell was embarked on authorship and was married, and Father Antoninus wrote to his wife:

> Once more I have to thank Wilfrid for his unceasing goodness to me. His handsome *Leo XIII* arrived safely this morning. If I convey my thanks to him through you I am sure they will be the more welcome. Of course you know that ever since I knew Wilfrid I have had a deep and special interest in him, and just now I seem to be reaping the consolation of a mother who witnesses the development of high attainments and noble virtues in her child. Wilfrid is the "Bravo figluolo" and I the "Vecchio Padrone" but there is a tender and a lasting love between us. And for this reason I am in some measure honoured by what he does.

Wilfrid in his teens was busy filling commonplace books with instances of touching virtue, such as those to be gathered from Mrs. Craven's *A Sister's Story*, and with quotations from the poets—the kind of commonplace books which were sure to be leading to manuscript books of his own tales of touching virtue, and of his own verses. John Bright was a friend of his father. A connection of John Bright was an Emily Priestman, "my first Catholic woman friend," Wilfrid Meynell labels her. She wrote *Simple Tales*. The tales were interleaved with verses by Wilfrid Meynell. The book was anonymous on the part of both authors, and was published by R. Washbourne in 1873. Children's deathbeds were then all too easily borrowed from fact to sentimentalize a story, and Mrs. Priestman, a tender and humane woman, drew on them, like better writers, for scenes of unnatural edification, bound to seem shocking to us now in their pious exploitation—and the narrative verses did the same in rhyme.

But young Meynell had his livelihood to get and this incident should hardly have encouraged him to think he could do it by means of his pen. His prolific juvenilia found a further outlet when in combination with his brother Philip—the one other literary member of the family of seven—and with a friend of his schooldays, Herbert Compton, a volume was produced of *Verses by Three Friends*. What was emerging in him was at any rate a considerable facility. But it was his own unwavering inclination, in advance of what there was to show, which governed his choice of a profession, and made him so exclusively the thing he was to become. He determined to set out for London. Few later allusions were made by him, in a life that swiftly unfolded, to the Newcastle days which he now left behind. But once when his second daughter visited Newcastle as a child he wrote to her from London:

I thought of you at St. Dominic's at 10 this morning. Were you there? How many happy tears have I shed in that church when, in my early youth, I had no other interest or attachment than those which belonged to the expression of religion. Now I have so many proxies of Heaven & of Christ—my dear home, your mother, you, & the rest of the family, that I sometimes think perhaps I seem to set too little store by church-going.

Into his story, on his arrival in London, a certain man now comes who was a decisive pointer to every direction the young man's life was to take. This was Father Lockhart (cousin of Scott's son-in-law and biographer), a member of the Order of the Institute of Charity founded by Rosmini. In 1838, when he was nineteen years of age, William Lockhart had gone up to Oxford and entered Exeter College as a commoner, and with his friends was preoccupied with leanings towards Catholicism. He was involved with both Manning and Newman in the conscience-storms then prevailing. Manning, Archdeacon of Chichester Cathedral, was a family friend, who warned Lockhart's mother, at that time of tension, against contact with her son when he had turned Catholic "as she valued her salvation." Thirty years later, as Archbishop Manning, he spoke of one of the priests of his diocese, who had long been his most earnest missioner, as "my dear friend Father Lockhart whom I have known as intimately as one man can know another."

It was to Newman at St. Mary's, Littlemore, that Lockhart as a hesitant young graduate on leaving Oxford went to be prepared for ordination in the Church of England, sent there by Manning in the belief that Newman would steady the young man's Anglican allegiance. Under the sway of Newman's learning and holiness, Lockhart remained a year at Littlemore; he left when he could no longer deny his own convictions. He was received into the Catholic Church and three days later became a postulant in the Institute of Charity. He was ordained in 1845. In the meantime "Mr. Newman," immediately after his own conversion, had paid "a most kind and loving visit" to the novitiate Brother Lockhart at Ratcliffe College.

In 1873 the Fathers of Charity were installed at St. Etheldreda's in Ely Place, Holborn, built at the end of the thirteenth century as a domestic chapel for the Bishops of Ely. Father Lockhart, now the rector, threw open the priests' house to young men who coming to work in London had no protecting home. He was a man of noble countenance and stature, an ardent preacher indoors and outdoors, the temperance reformer the times needed, and a journalist, editor of Catholic periodicals, and author. He held all the cues for Wilfrid Meynell to take up when he in his

4

turn found the doors of the priests' house open to him on his coming to London in his early twenties to seek a livelihood.

Meynell assisted in the work of the parish, and caught a life-long habit of being unable to pass a beggar without making a momentary friend of him. He shared the Fathers' habits of self-denial, and never abandoned them. He had a unique opportunity for an entry into Catholic journalism, and in the pages of *The Lamp*, edited by Father Lockhart, appeared his serial *Lost and Found, or the Story of a Girl's Life* (which all too inevitably proved to be the story of her death) with its now nostalgic illustrations of whiskered middle-aged-looking young men, and fichued and full-skirted young women swooning. There were also fluent verses by him, similarly illustrated. He became a constant scrib-bler. As journalist and editor he would outstrip Father Lockhart before long; in care for the unfortunate the model was unsur-passable, though Meynell could catch from him that complete brotherliness with the uncouth, the ragged, and the unpresentable, which when Francis Thompson crossed his path made him always uncritical of his outward condition. Through Lockhart, too, there was the significant introduction to Manning who in 1881 handed over to the young man the *Weekly Register* to own and to edit (when the rôles became reversed and Lockhart was con-tributor under his protégé's editorship).

It was above all through Lockhart that Meynell met his future wife. In 1876 he was twenty-four, a young man of middle height, blue-eyed, with the roman nose of all his family, clean-shaven, and not very correctly clothed. He fell in love with a sonnet by Alice Thompson[1] quoted in a review in the *Pall Mall Gazette* of her first volume of poems called *Preludes*. Father Lockhart knew her mother and introduced the young man to one of her after-noon musical at-homes. He became a regular caller, and frequent letters between "My dear Mr. Meynell" and "My dear Miss Thompson" were exchanged, he being a fervent sonneteer, she

---

[1] The maiden name of Meynell's wife and that of his friend Francis Thomp-son being the same, people have been sometimes misled into thinking they were related.

his critic. Eight months after their first meeting they were engaged. Father Lockhart wrote to her:

St. Etheldreda's,
14 Ely Place,
Holborn, E.C.
Jan. 1, 1877.

My dear Child,
I will not let an hour pass without expressing my deep sympathy in all I have heard today. It has wholly taken me by surprise. It has however confirmed the opinion I had formed of you and of your sister that you were unworldly and unspoiled by the praise of the world. You have determined to link your lot with one who is chivalrous in honour, tender in pity and love and who will be faithful to the end and true as steel in weal and woe. For him you have been willing to forgo a more brilliant but not as I believe a happier lot. My only anxiety is to know that you have your father's and mother's blessing.
May God bless you both.

Yours affectionately,
W. L.

It is just possible to decipher the now-faded ink in which she replied in her beautiful hand the next day.

Dear Reverend Father,
Many thanks for your blessing. My future husband will I am sure make me a better woman than I have been hitherto. With kindest regards and good wishes for the New Year, Believe me, dear Reverend Father,

Respectfully and gratefully yours,
Alice Thompson

Her father's blessing was conspicuously lacking. He was Thomas James Thompson, a close friend of Dickens, and a widower when he married Christiana Weller. He had no profession, was fond of travel, and had himself been responsible for their two daughters' education. Alice Thompson's letters to her betrothed written daily in the first months of 1877 reflect the

6

difficult situation. "The project about the *Lamp* I certainly like,[1] but you know this could only be one of other things. My father would never consent to my marriage with nothing to trust in but that. Don't be hurt or discouraged, will you? Trust to my constancy. . . ." "My father is calmer, he speaks of you with the esteem which you can never fail to win. Write him one of your own charming letters; let him see something of your heart." "Why are you so unhappy? It breaks my heart. I give you my word of honour to wait for a year if we cannot marry sooner. I would say more if I might. I gave a promise to Papa that I would not make an indefinite engagement, and I will be true to the letter of this promise, but not beyond." "I think I have conquered my father by force of obedience and unchanged affection. He spoke to me kindly this morning and the clouds are lifting." "I left Father Lockhart to tell you about last night, and indeed I was not present at his interview with my father. The *only* difficulty seems to be a financial one." "Mimi[2] today suggested the very thing which Father Lockhart had thought of—a magazine to which she could contribute—not continually but often enough to make her drawings its speciality. I think it would be a delightful employment for us both to edit and write for this magazine. Would we not make it good? Mimi had always refused the many applications which had been made to her for illustrations, so that I did not take up this idea of Father Lockhart's until she herself mooted it." "I have set my heart on having *great* names in it. I aspire to Tennyson and to Matthew Arnold. Alfred Austin may write prose but he shall *not* twang that banjo Browning speaks of in our pages. Mivart shall write for us, not on poetry, nor on love (which he told me last summer was the only subject which *really* interested him) but on comparative anatomy. It is too delightful and exciting. . . . Austin Dobson shall give us some of his really charming

[1] Father Lockhart in his anxiety to help wished to hand over to Meynell the editorship of the *Lamp* for the benefit of its small salary; he also suggested a possible "readership" at the publishing house of Burns and Oates, which came to nothing then.

[2] Her sister Elizabeth, already famous in her girlhood as a painter of battle-scenes.

vers de société. And my dear Ruskin? Wilfrid, we will start *magnificently*." "Papa has had a kind of relapse into displeasure as to our engagement. He sent for me last night to ask me to break it quite off, but I told him I was pledged for a year." "I *do* like Pen and Pencil [a proposed name for their magazine] (failing anything more original). Today I write to Ruskin!" "I think *Pen and Pencil* will not do. I mentioned it to Mrs. Lane Clark, a well-read woman, and she exclaimed that it has been used again and again." "Alas, I have a disappointment for you, my poor boy. By this evening's post came a nasty crabbed crushing letter from Ruskin, putting an end to every shadow of a hope that he will write for us. It is a complete snubbing and not a very gentle one. He takes up the word 'Review' which I used instead of 'magazine' and harps upon it all through the letter. He is very glad I am engaged, but very sorry I am going to be a reviewer, as it is a profession impossible to follow with honour unless I were an *arch-angel* and he will not 'go beyond angel even for me.' He then adds that I ought to have guessed his feeling on the subject, and ends by wishing me a happy marriage 'and a better trade.' " "The failure of Ruskin makes it all the more necessary to get at Browning, don't you think so? Dear Wilfrid, I feel so unhappy this morning. I should like to hide my tears on your shoulder and I cannot." "Mama told me that Papa had received a 'sweet little note' from Father Lockhart which seemed to touch him, and which made her cry."

A small allowance was made by their families to each of them, and the marriage edged its way into general acceptance. "The sixteenth be it!" Alice writes at the end of March, 1877, referring to the following month. "White dress, four bridesmaids, and a limited family breakfast. I will accept the offer of your sister's providing her dress, dear Wilfrid, if she does not mind. I have rather a panic about my bullion. Will you please tell her that the dresses are of white cachemine with revers of rose-coloured silk, white plush hats lined with rose colour, and that the dress must fasten *down the front*. Particulars as to style and a specimen of the colours I will send her." "Papa has been *too* kind. [She had been confined to bed.] He has hardly left me and it was touching to see how he stuck up my brass things [wedding presents] in sight of the bed to amuse me."

The marriage was performed by the Bishop of Nottingham at the Church of the Servite Fathers in Fulham Road. The bride wore round her neck the gold rosary of Mary Queen of Scots, an heirloom in the bridegroom's family. Father Lockhart wrote to Meynell from St. Etheldreda's: "The house seems strange without you—and I can hardly realise that you have flown from your little nest."

At 11 Inkerman Terrace, Kensington, next door to Alice's parents, the young couple set up house, both working at journalism, and in 1880 without an office embarked on their first editorship. *The Pen, a Journal of Literature* survived only for seven weekly appearances. A letter from Dante Gabriel Rossetti to Frederick Shields says: "I think I told you that a thing called *The Pen* had descanted flatteringly upon me, as I heard. I have since seen it, and it is very good (I know not by whom at all), but I regret to find that I have killed off *The Pen*, as its writing days ceased with that number."

But there was nothing abortive about the *Weekly Register* which in the next year, 1881, was handed over to Meynell by Archbishop Manning, in the thirty-second year of its age, and which now found a skilful and rejuvenating editor. *The Weekly Register, a Catholic Family Newspaper. Price threepence, post free. Published at 3 o'clock every Friday afternoon, by John Sinkins, at 43 Essex Street, Strand*—that is the summary of the task, earning an average profit of £300 a year, which was going to occupy and support both husband and wife for eighteen years, with friends hurrying to the rescue in proof-reading and filling space-gaps when pressure of other work or illness made a crisis. The *Register*, liberal-minded, was the friendly rival of the more conservative *Tablet*. Frequent visits by the editor to Manning for guidance on matters of policy made him the Cardinal's fervent young friend.

But the *Weekly Register* with its thirty-two pages was a Catholic newspaper, devoted to diocesan and parochial events, reports

9

from churches, colleges, and schools, conference reports and correspondence, news from Rome. For an editor who was an enthusiastic layman and had now proved himself a born journalist this was very well as far as it went, but literature and art were left in the lurch—and that was insupportable. *Merry England* had to come, and it was started in 1883. It could avail itself of *Weekly Register* facilities for printing and publishing. At first Meynell owned it conjointly with Messrs. Burns and Oates, but this firm retired from the partnership at the end of the first year, leaving him sole proprietor. The profits in a typical year, 1891, without allowing for an editorial fee, were £37 15s. 9d. It survived for twelve years.

It was a shilling monthly, illustrated. It received a warm welcome throughout the Press (not least from the *Weekly Register*!). Its manifesto had high hopes. It began:

> Professor Ruskin does not love the steam plough, yet surely the steam plough in the midst of scenery the most idyllic is a better alternative—where such alternative must be—than a starving people. The Professor indeed supposes that the modern ploughboy's whistling, as well as his work, will be done by steam; but we have faith that the rustic will yet again whistle for himself, albeit no longer for "want of thought." Frankly accepting the conditions of Modern England, we would have it a Merry England too.

And it ended:

> In religion, as in literature, in art and in sociology, we shall seek to fulfil Dr. Johnson's precept and "clear our minds of cant"—the cant of commerce and the cant of capital, the cant even of chivalry and of labour, the cant of mediaevalism no less than the cant of modern days.

It was something new in Catholic literature, and was not confined to Catholic writers. George Saintsbury wrote in the first number on the Young England Movement. Hilaire Belloc, Lionel Johnson, Coventry Patmore, W. H. Hudson, Wilfrid Blunt, Aubrey de Vere, were among the magazine's contributors. But those who wrote most were the editor and his wife. A further in-the-family element was added by illustrations by Elizabeth Thompson, who was now the wife of William Butler, and by Butler's own historical and fictional contributions.

When he became an old man Meynell wrote to an unknown American Dominican nun answering enquiries concerning the inauguration of *Merry England* and the identification of the many pen-names used in it:

My dear Sister,
. . . I felt the need of an organ to put forward Catholic principles especially in regard to the redemption of the workers. Cardinal Manning's articles were nearly half-a-century ahead of his time. I got three or four friends to help, by putting down one hundred pounds each, to add to mine. One was my brother-in-law, Sir William Butler, and another was the Marquis of Ripon, a convert to the church, a very typical Englishman and at the time Viceroy of India. We spent little, as there was no editorial fee, and our contributions were many of them voluntary. Besides my pen-name of "John Oldcastle," to break the monotony I sometimes signed Francis Phillimore,[1] and when I edited and adapted two or three anonymous articles published in Catholic magazines a hundred years earlier I gave them the signature A. C. Opie (which meant a copy). Looking over some old volumes of *Merry England* . . . I see I used A. C. Opie also for articles that were the entire work of that great dullard but your devoted

Wilfrid Meynell

Five thousand copies of the first number were sold immediately. One subscriber and even contributor to the magazine was a certain Edward Healy Thompson of Manchester. He was a man whose misfortune it was to have a good-for-nothing and (secretly) opium-eating nephew, described by him as "a great trouble and sorrow to his father from his want of ballast. He started with every advantage, but has come to nothing. . . . There does not appear to

---

[1] The Meynells, with an increasing young family, had now moved to Upper Phillimore Place, still in Kensington.

have been anything of what is usually termed immorality; but he was never to be depended on, and I fear he indulged in drink." This young man who was the despair of his family was an extensive reader in wide fields; Aeschylus and Blake lived in his untidy pocket; to those around him he was the idle dreamer; and it was by means only of the written word that his life had any intimates. His visits to the disapproving Edward Healy Thompson could be fruitful of little but incompatible interchange between them. But he glanced at *Merry England* on his uncle's table, and in those pages met his future friend.

II

FRANCIS THOMPSON had been born in 1859 at Preston in Lancashire, the second son of Charles Thompson and Mary Turner Morton, his wife—their first child, a son, dying at one day old. He had two sisters, Polly and Maggie. Charles Thompson was a doctor and like his wife a convert to the Catholic Church. In 1864 the doctor moved to Ashton-under-Lyme, Francis's home from a child to manhood. When he was eleven he was sent to Ushaw College near Durham. He was of the kind to suffer most from the worst of school life, one of whom it could be said that he was never a schoolboy—only a boy at school. In later years he wrote of the persecution which overclouded Shelley's schooldays:

Of that persecution's effect upon him he has left us, in the *Revolt of Islam*, a picture which to many or most people very probably seems a poetical exaggeration; partly because Shelley appears to have escaped physical brutality, partly because adults are inclined to smile tenderly at childish sorrows which are not caused by physical suffering. That he escaped for the most part bodily violence is nothing to the purpose. It is the petty malignant annoyance recurring hour by hour, day by day, month by month, until its accumulation becomes an agony; it is this which is the most terrible weapon that boys have against their fellow boy, who is powerless to shun it because, unlike the man, he has virtually no privacy. His is the torture which the ancients used when they anointed their victim with honey and exposed him naked to the restless fever of the flies. He is a little St. Sebastian, sinking under the incessant flight of shafts which skilfully avoid the vital parts. We do not, therefore, suspect Shelley of exaggeration: he was no doubt in terrible misery. Those who think otherwise must forget their own past.

Francis's parents, in sending him to Ushaw, hoped he might enter the priesthood, but though he found favour with the authorities as a clever and docile boy they considered that his nervous timidity, indolence, and absent-mindedness debarred him from the vocation. It was a decision finally arrived at between Francis and the President after long and confidential deliberations. At eighteen he returned to his parents. He had been seven years at Ushaw: for the next six years he was a medical student at Owens College, Manchester, whither he went daily from Ashton-under-Lyme. In his preliminary examination he distinguished himself in Greek, but "I hated my scientific and medical studies," he wrote later, "and learned them badly. Now even that reluctant knowledge has grown priceless to me." Unknown to his father, he defaulted from his lectures, failed to work, read poetry in public libraries, visited museums and galleries. At odds with his surroundings and occupation, his eccentricities grew upon him, and he has been described by a neighbour there as taking his walks "up Stalybridge Road and in the semi-rural outskirts of Ashton . . . the quick short step, the sudden and apparently causeless hesitation or full stop, then the old quick pace again, the continued muttering soliloquy, the frail and slight figure."

During his medical studentship he fell ill of a long fever, which probably caused his introduction to laudanum. In accordance with his literary tastes, his mother gave him about this time a copy of de Quincey's *Confessions of an English Opium Eater*. So great was the impact of this other Manchester alien upon young Thompson, and the similarity of experience, now and to come, and the likeness in their separateness from their fellows and in their rare and robust vocabularies, that it has been remarked that in giving him de Quincey it was as if Mrs. Thompson had found for him a guardian or spokesman or borne him an elder brother. She died not long after making this fateful gift.

Thompson made little headway with his medical studies. It is not known for certain that he actually sat for the two examinations for which he went to London in four years, and of which he merely reported to his father that he had not passed: he may

14

simply have absented himself from them. But on making enquiries at Owens College as to the cause of the failures, Dr. Thompson had the unpleasant shock of learning of his son's high rate of non-attendance at lectures. He was not without leniency. But the state of things was as painful to father and son as must be any maladjustment long persisted in. A Glasgow degree was supposed to be easier of access, and thither Francis was sent. On his failure there his father lost heart and hope; he had spent much money on college fees; his son must be brought to the reality of working and earning. For two weeks Francis assisted in a surgical-instrument-maker's business; for two months he acted as purveyor of an encyclopaedia. In the background loomed the last resort of enlistment. And this was what it came to. He enlisted, was measured, marched and drilled and then rejected as below the army physical standard.

On a Sunday in November, 1885, in an interview between father and son to explore the dark future, Dr. Thompson voiced the most pained suspicion of all—that his son was drinking. It was an accusation Francis could deny; that he was taking opium was his own secret. His father was a kind man: this alienation and deceit were what Francis could no longer endure. On the following day he left a note on his sister's dressing-table saying that he was going to London. He never had a home again.

He went first to Manchester and lingered there for a week. He was used to selling his books and medical instruments to buy laudanum; he now sold nearly every precious book he possessed, but still had to write home for his fare to London, dating from a Manchester post office. The fare was sent.

He arrived in London. He was in his twenty-sixth year, a hesitant young man with a slight Lancashire accent (the vowel sound in the word "book" he pronounced the same as in the word "boon"), thin, sloping-shouldered, of medium height with a gentle voice even before it became tremulous, and eyes with something of beauty when their strong straight look was not dazed. Experience in London opened with a job at a bookseller's. His part was to collect from publishing houses the books required by the bookseller each day, and these he carried in a sack. In addition to his pay he had seven shillings a week, sent by his father to be called for at a reading-room in the Strand. When therefore his employment by the bookseller soon came to an end there was still a shilling a day until the next job was found, and the next.

The thing which must most govern the condition of the vagrant worker is where he can afford to spend his night. In the daytime he may achieve normality of occupation. But where does he sleep?

It is not known where Thompson lodged on his arrival, but he may have started well enough. The decline came inevitably with gaps in employment, gaps which he did not always hasten to fill, pulled by the attraction of the Guildhall Library. There was an ample choice of beds at a shilling a night, and no doubt he found by experience which of them was the least objectionable. But there were stretches of time when a sixpence for holding a horse's head was his only earning. He tried a boot-black stand but was moved on by the police at the request of the shopkeeper at the street corner where he had his pitch. At such times there was no money for a bed of any kind, and he slept in a shelter or on the embankment. The Shelter was as it were society's or Charity's minimum safeguard against any man or woman being obliged to sleep out of doors, and as such it must have been some kind of boon; he lay then in an oblong box without a lid, fitted with a mattress; the cover was a leather apron. What will-less drifting led him sometimes instead to a bench open to the weather on the embankment can be known only to those who have lost the power of making decisions.

Sir Osbert Sitwell, in his Introduction to *Collected Poems* of W. H. Davies, writes:

. . . One cold and wet evening Davies was sitting on a broken wooden box near a large brazier in a Lambeth doss-house. In spite of the suffocating fumes it emitted he was reading by the glow of it, for there was no light. The general noise and rowdiness were insupportable, for it was Saturday night, and everyone who could, or could not, afford it had got

16

drunk. In the whole room he was the only quiet man, except for a mysterious stranger who sat opposite and talked to nobody. He, too, was trying to read, and something in the look of him made Davies wonder who he was. Indeed, he would have liked to enter into conversation, but the man seemed wrapped in his book, or else in melancholy thoughts, and a sort of shyness and restraint came over Davies. Many years later, however, when he consented to take part in a reading by famous modern poets, he saw there, again, on the platform, the stranger of the Lambeth doss-house. It was Francis Thompson.

Two poets in one doss-house would have been interesting, but there is a bar to accepting the incident as it stands, for it is certain that Thompson was never a famous modern poet reading his poems on a platform.

Sleeping out or under an archway was what clinched the disaster to his appearance. He had tried to preserve the looks of a man eligible for a job or presentable at a public library. His uncleanliness and ragged clothes soon made him unacceptable in any regular employment. The habit of such vagrants was to run behind hansoms or four-wheel cabs on which there was luggage, to earn some coppers by unloading the trunks at the unforeseeable end of the journey. Thus those who could least run ran this impossible race and if they were lucky lifted weights under which their thin bodies staggered. Match-selling was better. Such chances of the streets were Francis's semi-livelihood.

It is a curious fact that he ceased to collect his father's seven shillings—though not so curious perhaps to one who remembers his constant minor shortcomings later, covered by the repetitive half-plausible excuses: I was late, I was ill, I mistook the hour, the day, the week. For between him and the plainest doings there could be a barrier of effort or even fear. If that had been the age of the Welfare State he would have escaped its benefits. After a while the uncollected money was sent no more. He had besides relations in London to whom he might make an appeal, but did not.

In the doss-houses where he made his tea he met with generosity among the nameless crew who were his fellows; he said "only once did anyone try to cheat me." In a notebook he makes reference to the man among them whom they believed to be a murderer. Prison had no sound of disgrace. But the talk of some revolted him. He came from a pious home, and had round his neck the holy medal he still wore when he died. The incongruities of street-life were of many different kinds. A policeman once gave him an alms.

A beneficence which had far-reaching results happened in August, 1886. Thompson had been nearly nine months in London. His existence was made of unexpressed poetry, delirium, misery, starvation, and rags. He was wandering through Wardour Street when he was stopped and addressed by a man. Unlike most of the strange incidents which must be scattered about the days of anyone living outside society, this one did not pass at once into indifferent oblivion.

Mr. McMaster was a bootmaker, his shop being at 14 Panton Street, Haymarket. He was a Church of England man, a church-councillor and church-warden, and a man with a missionary zeal. It was his custom on meeting with a vagrant in the street to ask him if his soul was saved, perhaps identifying his misfortunes with his moral character. When Thompson heard the somewhat crude approach that day he rebuffed the stranger as having no right to question him. Mr. McMaster had however only been putting first things first. He said: "If you won't let me save your soul let me save your body." He had rescues to his credit, at that time when vagrancy was common, and a pauper of his would be taught a trade and even to sing in the choir at St. Martin's church. He was a simple, sincere man and Thompson submitted to his will.

McMaster decided to employ Thompson in his shop, but he first wrote to the superintendent of police at Ashton-under-Lyme for confirmation of his statement that he was the son of Dr. Charles Thompson of that place. Satisfied, he installed Thompson in a lodging in Southampton Row, newly clothed him, and introduced him into the shop, chiefly as messenger to deliver goods. He was given his food and lodging and five shillings a week. McMaster realized that Thompson as a Catholic was not a subject

18

for his own particular brand of hearty missionizing, but "not a bit of difference!" he claimed, in speaking of it in later days, did that make; and the repeated "not a bit of difference!" was to the credit of the churchman. He knew that Thompson recited prayers, and, getting it a bit wrong, recalled that "he said his Mass—always said his Mass—every night."

The new recruit was a listless messenger, but with McMaster he had found good fortune. For McMaster was a reader, and lent him books; he was also, and his father too, a conversationalist; and in their living-room in Panton Street there were many interested discussions, and Thompson, he said, was "a great talker." Those who knew him later would agree that he was a great talker —a silent man who was a great talker; the silence was not ordinary, it was half unconsciousness; the talk could be mere prattle. At McMaster's, too, he had pen and paper, and he was writing both poetry and prose, and some of this was sent to magazines, without success.

Communication was reopened with his father, and after three months of this semi-redemption it was arranged that he should go home for Christmas. Thanks to McMaster he was in trim for the visit. And in spite of all he had experienced his family saw little change in him. They had heard from McMaster of his former destitution, but now it was a closed book between them. Dr. Thompson had long abandoned the hope of his son's being successful in anything; that he should hold some humble employment might be the most he was suited for.

McMaster had hoped that his family would help Thompson to pull himself together, for he himself was far from satisfied with him. But on Thompson's return to London from Ashton he performed his duties in the shop even less well than before. To McMaster's keen disappointment his protégé was not only more inept but his periods of complete uselessness, of which McMaster had learnt the on-coming symptoms of restlessness and flushes, and the subsequent peaceful half-oblivion, were more frequent. He concluded Thompson was drinking. He had done his best but he knew when he was beaten, and they parted in the middle of

January. When, years after, he was questioned, and deplored the issue of his efforts for Thompson, he used his disappointment for a legitimate boast: "He was my only failure."

To be surprised that Thompson should now retrogress to the life of the streets is to forget too soon the surprise that he should ever have fallen on that life. The same factors worked now as then. He was a misfit in any situation which life offered, and with nothing to hold him back the street-life happened; the reasons were inherent, he was following his bent—not towards anything, but away. It may be that the meagre affluence under McMaster had made opium more accessible and his downfall was therefore the more inevitable. He re-entered the underworld.

And again, in the accidents of the streets to which those are exposed who are never out of them, he met with succour which a last gasp seems to draw to itself. It was winter, and nights were terrible in the open. He was pitied by a girl who repeatedly took him home to her own lodging, to stay there, and to be warmed and fed. This strange relationship lasted until a new chapter of existence began for Francis, and then ended abruptly by her own disappearance without an address, so that he sought for her in vain. It is inevitable that the parallel with de Quincey should arise, the men coming from the same city to the same London destitution, with opium for their resource. De Quincey's familiar passage about Ann covers Thompson's experience.

Being myself, at that time, of necessity a peripatetic, or a walker of the streets, I naturally fell in more frequently with those female peripatetics who are technically called street-walkers. Some of these women had occasionally taken my part against watchmen who wished to drive me off the steps of houses where I was sitting; others had protected me against more serious aggressions. But one amongst them—the one on whose account to have at all introduced this subject—yet no! let me not class thee, O noble-minded Ann —, with that order of women; let me find, if it be possible, some gentler name to designate the condition of her to whose bounty and compassion—ministering to my necessities when all the world stood

20

aloof from me—I owe it that I am at this time alive. For many weeks I had walked, at nights, with the poor friendless girl up and down Oxford Street, or had rested with her on steps and under the shelter of porticos. She could not be so old as myself: she told me, indeed, that she had not completed her sixteenth year. . . . The generous girl, without a murmur, paid out of her own humble purse, at a time, be it remembered, when she had scarcely wherewithal to purchase the bare necessaries of life, and when she could have no reason to expect that I should ever be able to reimburse her. O youthful benefactress! how often in succeeding years, standing in solitary places, and thinking of thee with grief of heart and perfect love—how often have I wished that, as in ancient times the curse of a father was believed to have a supernatural power, and to pursue its object with a fatal necessity of fulfilment, even so the benediction of a heart oppressed with gratitude might have a like prerogative; might have power given it from above to chase, to haunt, to waylay, to pursue thee into the central darkness of a London brothel, or (if it were possible) even into the darkness of the grave, there to awaken thee with an authentic message of peace and forgiveness, and of final reconciliation!

Their secretive trade strips them of name or biography, and nothing of either girl can be known except their transient kindness which achieved permanence. It was when Thompson came to address a poem to a child he loved, in *Sister Songs,* that *his* confession of an opium-eater commemorated *his* Ann, for with the child he was addressing in the poem he linked the childishness of the girl he had known.

> Forlorn, and faint, and stark
> I had endured through watches of the dark
>   The abashless inquisition of each star,
> Yea, was the outcast mark
>   Of all those heavenly passers' scrutiny;
>   Stood bound and helplessly
> For Time to shoot his barbèd minutes at me;
> Suffered the trampling hoof of every hour
>   In night's slow-wheelèd car;

Until the tardy dawn dragged me at length
From under those dread wheels; and, bled of strength,
　I waited the inevitable last.
　Then there came past
A child; like thee, a spring-flower; but a flower
Fallen from the budded coronal of Spring,
And through the city streets blown withering.
She passed,—O brave, sad, lovingest, tender thing!
And of her own scant pittance did she give,
　That I might eat and live:
Then fled, a swift and trackless fugitive.
　Therefore I kissed in thee
The heart of Childhood, so divine for me;
　And her, through what sore ways
　And what unchildish days
Borne from me now, as then, a trackless fugitive.
　Therefore I kissed in thee
　Her, child! and innocency.

The lengthening period of nothing but a sixpenny kind of employment made his ill-condition progressive. There died in him the idea that he might have the power to write; any attempt to justify such an idea had failed. In February, 1887, in some interlude in misfortune, as he noted later, "with a few shillings to give me breathing-space I began to decipher and put together ye[1] half-obliterated rough Ms. of *Paganism*. I came simultaneously to my last page & last halfpenny; & went forth to drop ye Ms. in *M.E.* Next day I spent the halfpenny on two boxes of matches, and began ye struggle for life." With the MS. he sent a covering letter, giving a Charing Cross post-office address.

He had now a hope, for almost against nature he had accomplished something, and he believed that in the pages of *Merry England* there might be a place for him if anywhere. But the days and weeks went by and there was no answer from *Merry England*, and the hope was gone. Hardships were having increasing effect. The second year in London was bound to tell harder on him than

[1] Thompson habitually used y, the graphic variant of the Old English letter thorn, for "th" in the word "the."

the first; in the third it seemed that his accumulated ills could have only one end—an end which he may even have been in danger of hastening by his own act. Wilfrid Blunt, in Part Two of *My Diaries*, published in 1919, relates under the date of August, 1907, that Wilfrid Meynell described to him the circumstances of Thompson's street-life, including his sleeping at night under the arches of Covent Garden. Of what Blunt then proceeds to quote from Meynell there is no other record by Meynell himself; he may have been reluctant to make it common knowledge.

It was in an empty space of ground behind the market where the gardeners throw their rubbish that he had resolved on suicide. He spent all his remaining pence on laudanum, one large dose, and he went there one night to take it. He had swallowed half when he felt an arm laid on his wrist, and looking up he saw Chatterton standing over him and forbidding him to drink the other half. I asked him when he told me of it how he had known that it was Chatterton. He said, "I recognised him from the pictures of him—besides, I knew that it was he before I saw him."

III

THE packet dropped into the letter-box of *Merry England* was pigeon-holed by Meynell. Six months later he examined it.

The mention of a pigeon-holed MS. immediately evokes the memory of the sea of papers which flooded the family-life of the journalist-author-editor, and his extensive measures to control them. All his life he was a great keeper, but much of the stowing away was the prelude to a life-long parting. When in 1889 he had a house built in Palace Court the carpentry in the library was designed for the maximum accommodation of papers, and the eighteen feet of deep lockers under the windows held such vast layers as to amount to burial. Ingenious pigeon-holes had each its little shutter or door framing a portrait which showed at a glance who was the subject concerned. In addition there were nests of small drawers, the subject-matter written outside. Scores of book-boxes were in the shelves, also with name or newspaper portrait on each. Even so, the papers lying always on the long table were inches deep, affording good cover for a missing document.

The length of the parting with the papers he stowed away is proved when to-day letters are brought to light which have not been touched since he put them in their place. In many the flaps have restuck themselves and are opened as if for the first time. One letter, moved for the first time since 1879, is representative of a few others showing what could sometimes happen. It is from Sir Laurence Alma Tadema. Meynell, in the early days of his ubiquitous journalism, was doing editorial work on the *Art Journal*, and this artist was asked for a certain piece of information about his work, and it irritated him that he had to send it twice.

His annoyance is perhaps robbed of its perfect effect by mis-spelling. His letter begins

Dear Mr. Meynell,
    Editors ought not to loose business letters,

before he repeats the information.

The infinite keeping comprised newspaper cuttings for reference purposes. It is difficult to remember seeing him read a newspaper without his tearing something out. He must have been one of the busiest journalists in London, writing for many papers besides the two of his own, and he could not afford to consider that any subject was outside his scope. He dovetailed one thing in with another in a pressure which extended to his actual movement; his fast walk to office or printer was apt to break into a half-gliding trot, of which another of the early letters is a reminder, his friend, St. George Mivart, who was always seeking a meeting with him, writing that he had seen him in the street "but you were running so I thought it better not to stop you."

The pigeon-holed Francis Thompson packet, when it was finally examined, was of an appearance to depress expectation; the covering letter was written on a piece of murky paper, never intended for letter-paper, as small as half the size of a single sheet of that, and allowing no space for a margin.

February 23/87.
Dear Sir,
    In enclosing the accompanying article for your inspection, I must ask pardon for the soiled state of the manuscript.   It is due, not to slovenliness, but to the strange places and circumstances under which it has been written. For me, no less than Parolles, the dirty nurse Experience has something fouled. I enclose stamped envelope for a reply, since I do not desire the return of the manuscript, regarding your judgment of its worthlessness as quite final. I can hardly expect that where my prose fails my verse will succeed. Nevertheless, on the principle of "yet will I try the last," I have added a few specimens of it, with the off-chance that one may be less poor than the rest.

Apologising very sincerely for any intrusion on your valuable time, I remain,

Yours with little hope,

Francis Thompson

Kindly address your rejection to the Charing Cross Post Office.

The essay and one of the poems seemed worthy of acceptance, and the now sixth-month-old letter aroused curiosity. Meynell wrote to Charing Cross post office asking Thompson to call at *Merry England* office to see a proof and discuss future work. There was no reply. Time which moves at so different a pace for different people flew by month after month for the occupied editor before the question of Francis Thompson again came in for the amount of attention that means action. In April, 1888, Meynell printed in *Merry England* one of the poems, "The Passion of Mary," hoping by this means to hear from the author. The idea succeeded.

April 14th, 1888.

Dear Sir,

In the last days of February or the first days of March, 1887 (my memory fails me as to the exact date), I forwarded to you for your magazine a prose article ("Paganism Old & New," or "Ancient & Modern," for I forget which wording I adopted) and accompanied it by some pieces of verse, on ye chance that if ye prose failed, some of ye verses might meet acceptance. I enclosed a stamped envelope for a reply, since (as I said) I did not desire ye return of ye manuscript. Imprudently, perhaps, instead of forwarding ye parcel through ye post, I dropped it with my own hand into ye letter-box of 43 Essex Street. There was consequently no stamp on it, since I did not think a stamp would be necessary under ye circumstances. I asked you to address your answer to ye Charing Cross Post Office. To be brief, from that day to this, no answer has ever come into my hands. And yet, more than twelve months since ye forwarding of ye manuscript, I am now informed that one of the copies of verse which I submitted to you (*i.e.* "The Passion of Mary") is appearing in this month's issue of *Merry England*. Such an occurrence I can only explain to myself in one way, viz., that some untoward accident cut off your means of communicating with me. To suppose otherwise—to suppose it intentional— would be to wrong your known honour and courtesy. I have no doubt that your explanation, when I receive it, will be entirely satisfactory to me. I therefore enclose a stamped and addressed envelope for an answer, hoping that you will recompense me for my long delay by the favour of an early reply. In any case, however long circumstances may possibly delay your reply, it will be sure of reaching me at the address I have now given.

I remain,

Yours respectfully,

Francis Joseph Thompson

P.S. Doubtless, when I received no answer, I ought to have written again. My excuse must be that a flood-tide of mis-fortune rolled over me, leaving me no leisure to occupy myself with what I regarded as an attempt that had hopelessly failed. Hence my entire subsequent silence.

The disreputable appearance of this letter belies the dignity of its wording; the paper is irredeemably dirty, the writing a scrawl, unlike the neat copperplate of his normal hand. The en-closed envelope bore the name of a chemist's shop in Drury Lane. Meynell sent there a letter by special messenger and after some days of silence went himself to the shop. The chemist knew little of Thompson; he might or might not call for a letter; he owed three-and-ninepence, which Meynell paid. The chemist promised to try to produce him. And after many days Thompson came to Essex Street. He wavered at the door of the editor's work-room, unable to make up his mind to enter. Once inside he presented a figure more ragged than the average beggar's; he had no shirt under his coat, no socks, and his shoes were broken. The editor's idea of getting hold of someone who might prove a useful writer was sub-merged in compassion. This was a man in the last stages of want.

The first contact of two lives which were to be so joined was not very productive, but it had at least a basis for sympathy. On Thompson's side, there was long-standing approval from a dis-tance of Meynell's function; he wrote later: "He has in my

27

opinion—an opinion of long standing—done more than any man in these latter days to educate Catholic literary opinion I was myself virtually his pupil (and his wife's) long before I knew him." And on Meynell's part there was a natural disposition for immediate friendliness with anyone. He was now thirty-six years old, to Thompson's twenty-nine, and his existence was as teeming with work and friends and a large young family as the other's was empty—but ready human contacts were his way of life. His habit with strangers was to dispense with formalities. At the first handshake he always probed for some small scale of intimacy. A favourite immediate question: "What is the last book you have read?" was not in fact always a fertile one, for it is surprising what a blank of memory it can evoke! But he would hardly notice that, for at any rate his own kind of footing had been established. When he was old it did not matter how trivial was the question he aimed on a first sight, as long as it was further on the road of familiarity than a more normal opening, and "At what time did you get up this morning?" often served him as well as any other.

At this first interview with Thompson, Meynell spoke of the essay "Paganism Old and New" and said: "You must have had access to many books when you wrote it," but Thompson replied that he had had no books at the time, and that was where the essay failed. He made no confidence or complaint touching his state, and when he was asked to write more and to accept a small weekly sum for subsistence he refused the help, and the meeting ended negatively. But the writing-opening was for him like a possible key to true life, and the editor's friendliness had made its mark, for Thompson came again to the office, and subjects for *Merry England* articles were discussed, and he came again, and soon was introduced to the editor's home in Upper Phillimore Place.

But he did not come as one willing to leave one state and enter another. He would not go all the way to security, he preferred the chance of calling a cab; two and a half years had made that kind of job second nature; his reluctance to leave the streets was like other people's reluctance to leave a house they are used to.

The May and June numbers of *Merry England* printed his poem "Dream Tryst" and his "Paganism Old and New," and such publication was doubtless the best lure to a new life. And yet he wrote nothing more for six months. He was a physical wreck; his opium habit was either confided or discovered, but it was only after much persuasion that Meynell induced him to be examined by a doctor. The doctor's opinion was that he would not live, and that his death might be hastened if he were deprived of the drug. Meynell decided with Thompson that the risk should be taken in a private hospital; after that, Meynell's increasing influence prevailed on him to go and lodge with the monks at the Priory at Storrington in Sussex.

His letters from Storrington show the physical ills and the literary struggles of a man between two lives.

Storrington Priory,
Pulborough, Sussex.

Dear Mr. Meynell,

I am, as I expected to be, very ill just now; so that you must excuse me if I confine my letter to what is necessary.

In the first place, Mrs. Blackburn[1] spoke of forwarding me some boots. If you can do so I should be very much obliged; and I want to make a request which looks rather like a luxury, but which I believe to be a necessity in my present position. Can you send me a razor? I shall have to shave myself here, I think, & it would of course be a saving of expense in ye long run. Any kind of a razor would do for me; I have shaved with a dissecting-scalpel before now. . . . Finally, with regard to ye books which Mrs. Blackburn spoke of your sending. Do not let what I have said regarding my illness delay you in that. It is true I am not at present capable of writing; but it would be an absolute mercy to have any books. At present there is nothing to keep my mind from dwelling on itself. I may say I shall want even a Shakespeare for ye *Dublin* article, since I

---

[1] Mrs. Blackburn, an elderly widow, knew Thompson in London and at Pantasaph in Wales and at Crawley in Sussex. She was an experienced sub-editor and proof-reader, and assisted the Capuchin Fathers with their *Franciscan Annals*, and the Meynells with their papers when necessary. Thompson refers to her in later letters by her nickname, "Madam."

believe they have not one here. I wish they had. I could easily find distraction for my mind there. And with regard to my illness, there is nothing to be alarmed about. It is severer & more obstinate than I had hoped would be ye case, but it is a mere matter of holding on. And in that kind of passive endurance I am well practised. I daresay this week will see ye end of it.

I think I shall like this place when I begin again to like anything. The want of books is the principal drawback so far as I see at present. Let me say that I keep on my legs, & force myself to go out as much as possible. . . . And oh please when you send me anything, let me, if you can, have Mrs. Meynell's article which you promised I should have.

Yours very sincerely,
Francis Thompson

Please accept my warmest thanks for all your kindness & trouble on my behalf. I know this is a very perfunctory-looking letter; but until ye first sharp struggle is over, it is difficult for me to write in any other way.

Storrington Priory.

How good and kind and patient you are with me! far more than I am with myself, for I am often fairly sick of the being that inhabits this villainous mud-hut of a body. I received the medicine all right. I was, for four or five days, much better, but I am sorry to say that it did not last. Having noticed that the attacks came on principally during ye half-sleep of early night or early morning, I sat up ye greater part of ye night in order to tire myself into heavy sleep. The device was successful during ye four nights that I kept it up; but ye first night that weariness caused me to drop it, ye attack returned. I must, however, count it something gained that the consequences are no longer so severe as they were, & I have hopes that ye thing may gradually be loosening its hold upon me. I beguiled the four nights I have spoken of, while ye mental cloud was somewhat lifted, by writing ye verses I herewith send you. If there be no saving-grace of poetry in them, they are damned; for I am painfully conscious that they display me, in every respect, at my morally weakest. Indeed no one but yourself—or, to be more accurate, yourselves—would I have allowed to see them; for verse written as I write it is often nothing less than a confessional, a confessional far more intimate than ye sacerdotal one. *That* touches only your sins, and leaves in merciful darkness your ignominious, if sinless, weaknesses. If there be poetry in your verse, ye poetry may condone ye weakness; but if there be not—& that means nine times out of ten—it requires some confidence to give anyone ye opportunity of becoming acquainted with them. When ye soul goes forth, like Anderson's Emperor, thinking herself clothed round with singing-robes, while in reality her naked weakness is given defenceless to ye visiting wind, not every mother's son would you allow to gaze on you at such a time.

Storrington Priory.

The *Dublin* article having been sent, I write to ask you for more work, or directions as to work. I am afraid, however, that even if there is room for it, ye article will hardly be in time, & that through my own fault. I miscalculated the date. ... Even if I had known, though, I hardly think I could have finished it a day earlier, for I worked so badly to begin with. This is something like a confession of failure, and I am naturally chagrined about it. But I have one comfort from ye affair. I not only hope but think . . . that it has broken me to harness. You asked me to write frankly, & so I will tell you just how I have found myself get on with my work. At first I could not get on at all. I tried regularly enough to settle myself to writing, but my brain would not work. Then gradually, after long pushing, my brain began slowly to move. It has not gone very fast since nor gone willingly, but I have been able to make it go regularly. ... If I have indeed begun to acquire the power of working in the teeth of nerves and mood and bilious melancholy, then the fight is half fought. And I think I have. I want some more work now, lest if left to myself I may lose a habit scarcely acquired.

Reminiscent of this time of his emerging from the streets he was later to write:

> With faint and painful pulses was I lying,
>   Not yet discerning well
> If I had 'scaped, or were an icicle,
>   Whose thawing is its dying.

But at Storrington in fact he gained a foothold on the life that was to be his. The somewhat prosy letters show the progress made; it was shown more startlingly otherwise. Up till now Meynell had been the guardian—almost nurse—of a sick man with a submerged talent. One day—it was now the midsummer of 1889—he received from Storrington the manuscript of the "Ode to the Setting Sun." It is a poem native to the place where it was written, using in its prelude the circumstances of the cross erected in the monastery field, and the music in it being that of some passing itinerant musicians:

> O setting Sun, that as in reverent days
>   Sinkest in music to thy smoothèd sleep,
> Discrowned of homage, though yet crowned with rays,
>   Hymned not at harvest more, though reapers reap:
>
> For thee this music wakes not. O deceived,
>   If thou hear in these thoughtless harmonies
> A pious phantom of adorings reaved,
>   And echo of fair ancient flatteries!
>
> Yet, in this field where the Cross planted reigns,
>   I know not what strange passion bows my head
> To thee, whose great command upon my veins
>   Proves thee a god for me not dead, not dead!
>
> For worship it is too incredulous,
>   For doubt—oh, too believing-passionate!
> What wild divinity makes my heart thus
>   A fount of most baptismal tears ?—Thy straight
>
> Long beam lies steady on the Cross. Ah me!
>   What secret would thy radiant finger show ?
> Of thy bright mastership, is this the key ?
>   Is *this* thy secret, then ? And is it woe ?
>
> Fling from thine ear the burning curls, and hark
>   A song thou hast not heard in Northern day;
> For Rome too daring, and for Greece too dark,
>   Sweet with wild things that pass, that pass away!

And the poem thus enters on to its imaginative course, from a brain which showed itself teeming with the equipment for poetry. To the Meynells it was a revelation, even calling for action, and they took train to Sussex to congratulate Thompson.

In the way of prose from Storrington he was not less surprising. He had been seen at the Meynells' by Bishop (afterwards Cardinal) Vaughan, who had known him at Ushaw and who owned but did not edit the *Dublin Review*. He suggested that Thompson should submit an article to the editor. At Storrington, Thompson decided, though with misgivings, that Shelley should be the subject. "Until I was twenty-two Shelley was more studied by me than anyone else. At the same time I am exposed to the danger of talking platitudes, because so much has been written about Shelley of late years which I have never read," he wrote to Meynell.

The Shelley essay was not platitudinous. It was original, rich in comparison and allusion, the fruit of years of a man's various reading and thought—a man, though, who had been denied by a policeman admittance to a public library when his appearance suggested that begging could be his only motive for entering. What he asked for now in order to write was not a Shelley volume but a writing-pad—and in the MS. the quotations had the slight inaccuracies of non-copied ones. It was a shrewdly argued estimate of man and poet—in language liable to burst the bonds of prose into flight and fancy. He spoke of looking behind Shelley's "wild mask of revolutionary metaphysics" to find a child's face, and his poetry the poetry of make-believe, typified in the purely Shelleian "The Cloud."

The same thing is conspicuous throughout his singing; it is the child's faculty of make-believe raised to the *nth* power. He is still at play, save only that his play is such as manhood stops to watch, and his playthings are those which the gods give their children. The universe is his box of toys. He dabbles his fingers in the day-fall. He is gold-dusty with tumbling amidst the stars. He makes bright mischief with the moon. The meteors nuzzle their noses in his hand. He teases into growling the kennelled thunder, and laughs at the shaking of its fiery chain. He dances in and out of the gates of heaven: its floor is littered with his broken fancies. He runs wild over the fields of ether. He chases the rolling world. He gets between the feet of the horses of the sun. He stands in the lap of patient Nature, and twines her loosened tresses after a hundred wilful fashions, to see how she will look nicest in his song.

Shelley's unhappiness is attributed again to childlike irrationality, "for no such hapless lot was Shelley's as that of his own contemporaries—Keats, half-chewed in the jaws of London and spit dying on to Italy; De Quincey, who, if he escaped, escaped rent and maimed from those cruel jaws; Coleridge, whom they dully mumbled for the major portion of his life." Nor was it due to unappreciation, or fears as to that "senseless superstition," the applause of posterity. "Posterity, posterity! which goes to Rome, weeps large-sized tears, carves beautiful inscriptions, over the tomb of Keats; and the worm must wriggle her curtsey to it all, since the dead boy, wherever he be, has quite other gear to tend. Never a bone less dry for all the tears."

The story of the Shelley essay Thompson tells at the time in a letter to an old friend of his family.

> The article on Shelley I finished at last, with quite agonising pain & elaboration. It might have been written in tears, & is proportionately dear to me. . . . It has not been inserted in the current issue of the *Dublin*—a fact which looks ominous. I prefaced it by a fiery attack on Catholic Philistinism, driven home with all the rhetoric which I could muster. That is pretty sure to be a stumbling-block. I consulted Mr. Meynell as to its suppression, but he said, "Leave it in." I suspect that he thoroughly agrees with it. . . . Mr. Meynell's opinion was " 'Shelley' is splendid." . . . There can now be no doubt that the *Dublin Review* has rejected my article. Nothing has been heard of it since it was sent. I only hope that they have not lost the Ms. That would be to lose the picked fruit of three painful months—a quite irreparable loss.

The essay was rejected and was put aside by Thompson among his few papers, where it lay till after his death.

IV

ALICE MEYNELL'S father having died in 1881 a sum of money had come to the Meynells with which they now decided to build a house. Their finances were to continue precarious in the extreme, a few shillings making the difference, in the week's budget, between solvency and debt (and the gift of £5 from an aunt at Christmas so essential that one year when it came late the parents' grave faces made the children know that all festivity hung on it). But throughout his life Meynell's moves were one step ahead of caution, and what appeared imprudent his industry then proceeded to justify. The house in Palace Court, Bayswater, designed by Leonard Stokes, gave expression to their own tastes, as likewise did the slowly collected Persian rugs and tiles and Morris furnishings. It was one of the first houses to be built in the wide street which was then a cul-de-sac closed by iron gates at the bottom. The site was bought in 1888 for £1,321; the building, completed in the following year, cost £2,426. Red-brick and gabled, its well-proportioned rooms comprised dining-room and morning-room on the ground floor, drawing-room and library on the next, with ten bedrooms and dressing-rooms above. It absorbed most of Alice Meynell's inheritance but it provided the space in which to bring up seven children, with Kensington Gardens close by for their playground.

The house was a hive of writing. Alice Meynell in this year, 1889, was writing essays beginning with "The Rhythm of Life" which the fastidious editor of the *National Observer*, W. E. Henley, called "one of the best things which it has so far been my privilege to print," and he was clamouring for more. Editorial work was shared in the library by husband and wife; there was no office staff; a devoted friend or two lent a hand if called upon. At the turn of the year it became obvious that Storrington, which had done much for Thompson, and meant much to him, was not what he needed now. He was ready to agree that he should have greater access to books and that for constant work as a journalist London was desirable. A lodging was found for him not far from Palace Court and he came there in February. He was in a condition when even the best for him was bad, and some time after leaving Storrington he wrote to the friend of his family:

> I must beg your and everybody's pardon for my long silence. The fact is that I have been for months in a condition of acute mental misery, frequently almost akin to mania, stifling ye production of everything except poetry, & rendering me quite incapable of sane letter-writing. It has ended in my return to London, & I am immensely relieved; for the removal of the opium had quite destroyed my power of bearing the almost unbroken solitude in which I found myself.

Already the chance of having saved him, the discovery of his powers, the gentle, helpless personality, and a general responsibility for him, were central parts of Meynell's existence. Thompson joined the workers at the library-table, where on Thursdays the pressure was at its height. He wrote reviews for the *Weekly Register* and prose and verse for *Merry England*, where, besides signing his own name, he shared the pen-names of the editor and his wife. Meynell wrote reminiscently: "Francis Tancred and Francis Phillimore were also the signatures of Francis Thompson and Alice Meynell. I forget whether I used Francis Tancred myself." They did this, he added, "thinking that readers would weary of the interminable repetition of our proper names."

Things were not easy-going. Thompson could not now, nor ever could, live according to the pattern of others. Trivially he was a disturbance at the busy table, making a tragic necessity of a different pen or paper and repetitively voicing the difficulties of the subject in hand. He was a great loser of the pencilled draft of his own compositions, carried about in the pocket of his ulster, and left on any handy surface. "It's a penny exercise-book," he repeatedly reminded the searchers, in a crisis of dismay. His lateness for an appointment was constitutional.

I called at Palace Court on Friday, and, finding you were gone, started to follow you. Unfortunately I fell into composition on the way, & when I next became conscious of matters sublunary, found myself wandering about somewhere in the region of Smithfield Market, & the time late in the afternoon. I am heartily sorry for my failure to keep my appointment, & hope you will forgive me. I thought I had disciplined myself out of these aberrations, which makes me feel all the more vexed about the matter. Always your F. T.

And sometimes his inability to conform overwhelmed him.

I wish you had never encumbered yourself with me. I am more in a condition to sit down & go into hysterics like a girl than to write anything. I know how vexed & impatient you must feel to hear this from me, when you had expected to have the thing from me this morning. Indeed I feel that you have already done too much for me; & that it would be better that you should have nothing more to do with me. You have already displayed a patience & tenderness with me that my kindred would never have displayed; & it is most unjust that I should any longer be a burden to you. I think I am fit for nothing: certainly not fit to be any longer the object of your too great kindness. Please understand that I entirely feel, & am perfectly resigned to the ending of an experiment which even your sweetness would never have burdened yourself with, if you could have foreseen the consequences.

F. T.

But he was, in this year of 1890 and the following two years, producing poetry which in 1893 would go into book form. Meynell was not only introducing him as a reviewer in more papers than his own, but this zeal made him active as a propagandist, and he had cherished the early contributions appearing in *Merry England* to the extent of sewing a few copies of them together to send to possible appreciators. A common friend sent one to Tennyson who merely answered through his son: "Dear Mr. Snead-Cox, Thanks for letting us see the vigorous poems. Yours truly, Hallam Tennyson." Browning, who was an occasional visitor at Palace Court, did otherwise, writing two months before his death:

Asolo, Veneto, Italia.
Oct. 7, '89.

Dear Mr. Meynell,

I hardly know how to apologise to you, or explain to myself how there has occurred such a delay in doing what I had an impulse to do as soon as I read the very interesting papers written by Mr. Thompson, and so kindly brought under my notice by yourself. Both the Verse and Prose are indeed remarkable—even without the particulars concerning their author, for which I am indebted to your goodness. It is altogether extraordinary that a young man so naturally gifted should need incitement to do justice to his own conspicuous ability by endeavouring to emerge from so uncongenial a course of life as that which you describe. Surely the least remunerating sort of literary life would offer advantages incompatible with the hardest of all struggles for existence, such as I take Mr. Thompson's to be. Pray assure him, if he cares to know it, that I have a confident expectation of its success, if he will but extricate himself—as by a strenuous effort he may—from all that must now embarrass him terribly. He can have no better friend and adviser than yourself—except *himself*, if he listens to the inner voice. Pray offer my best thanks to Mrs. Meynell for her remembrance of me—who am, as she desires, profiting by the quiet and beauty of this place—whence, however, I shall soon depart for Venice, on my way homeward. I gather, from the absence of anything to the contrary in your letter, that all is well with you—and so may it continue. I do not forget your old kindliness, though we are so much apart in London; and you must account me always, dear Mr. Meynell, as yours cordially,

Robert Browning

When Thompson saw this letter after Browning's death he wrote to Meynell:

. . . ye idea that in ye closing days of his life my writings should have been under his eye, & he should have sent me

38

praise & encouragement, is one that I shall treasure to ye closing days of *my* life. To say that I owe this to you is to say little. I have already told you that long before I had seen you, you exercised, unknown to myself, ye most decisive influence over my mental development when without such an influence my mental development was like to have utterly failed. And so to you I owe not merely Browning's notice, but also that ever I should have been worth his notice. The little flowers you sent him were sprung from your own seed. I only hope that ye time may not be far distant when better & less scanty flowers may repay ye pains, & patience, & tenderness of your gardening.

He was being given a place in life in lieu of nowhere. He possessed a family again, for his father was communicated with, and hearing his son was a poet said: "If the lad had but told me!" He was brought into things, however little he might seem to fit the part. The Meynell children were sent to skate on the Round Pond in his charge. He was made godfather to the youngest of them in 1891. All the Meynells' friends had to reckon with his presence; to some, notably Coventry Patmore, it proved as will be shown a meeting of utmost importance; the conventional were less edified. There was one man whose meeting with Thompson had its peculiar suitability, but of this neither showed any consciousness. This was the poet Lionel Johnson, as frail as Thompson himself, and as silent according to mood, and as like in some habits as to make it humorously obvious that if either wished to go to early Mass their only hope was not to go to bed the night before. But though Johnson, with his small body and fine delicate face, was named the Changeling in the Meynell family, and though he must have been as responsible as Thompson for the fact that they hardly spoke to each other, he was at times critical of that other changeling drooping in the chair close by. He wrote to his friend Imogen Guiney: "I have seen much of Francis Thompson at the Meynells lately; he enchants and exasperates me, both beyond measure, in his work and in himself. Patmore's self was, to me, exasperating; but there was genius in

39

his least tolerable moods and manners." But in these mixed feelings strong interest at any rate prevailed, and he addressed his poem "Sursum Corda" to Thompson, and his final summing-up of Thompson's poetry was finely expressed in a note written for Katharine Tynan, an interested person, since she, too, frequently saw Francis Thompson at the Meynells'.

Magnificently faulty at times, magnificently perfect at others. The ardours of poetry, taking you triumphantly by storm: a surging sea of verse, rising and falling and irresistibly advancing. Drunk with his inspiration, sometimes helplessly so: more often, he is merely fired and quickened, and remains master of himself. He has done more to harm the English language than the worst American newspapers: *Corruptio optimi pessima.* Has the opulent, prodigal manner of the seventeenth century; a profusion of great imagery, sometimes excessive and false: and another opulence and profusion, that of Shelley in his lyric choruses. Beneath the outward manner, a passionate reality of thought: profound, pathetic, full of faith without fear. "Words that, if you pricked them, would bleed," as was said of Meredith. Incapable of prettiness and pettiness: for good and bad, always vehement and burning and—to use a despised word—sublime. *Sublime*, rather than *noble*! too fevered to be austere: a note of ardent suffering, not of endurance.

Other friends of the Meynells to whom he was introduced were the Capuchin friars who had a monastery at Crawley in Sussex and one at Pantasaph in Wales. Among them were men admirably suited to Thompson. Father Cuthbert's opinion he felt compelled to seek for mystical enlightenment; the Provincial, Father Alphonsus, was one for whom Coventry Patmore's Odes made, as he said, a new heaven and a new earth. But it was to Father Anselm,[1] whom Thompson was to call his philosophical schoolmaster, and who had an outstanding personality of sweetness and grace, that he came nearest. A few extracts from Anselm's letters to Alice Meynell suggest the kind of man who off and on had much to do with Thompson. "I was unchristian enough to wish the author of *Christ in Hades* [Stephen Phillips]

[1] He became Archbishop of Simla in 1911.

40

to Hades itself, but only for a very brief period, that Sunday night I called. I like that young man, but I wanted to see more of you, & I didn't begin to be unchristian about him till he started to leave & then remained on. These gentlemen, said I, can come here every Sunday; but I—well, fancy the sentiments of a man, a holy Friar, whose sole intellectual pleasure is philosophy, & who knows that a woman can sometimes be a Summa Philosophica if not Theologica." "I hope the children got home safely & that they enjoyed their little sojourn in our village. My Crawley was sensitive to the going & coming of their dear feet, & for the moment we are lonelier without them." "I have a delightful recollection of our excursion in the fields where we plucked buttercups & where your unfrequenting voice lifted itself so gently in a few notes like those of a solemn bird over the little heads of the children on the grass. Do you remember?" From 1892 for ten years Anselm was the editor of the *Franciscan Annals*. He wrote to Meynell in 1897 "to thank you for your very kind & generous mention of our Magazine in the important columns of the *Academy*. I have always professed & still do profess that you are unquestionably our only Patriarch, Guide & Friend in the world of letters, & if our name has reached the finer circles of thought & action it is entirely through you and your peerless wife." In 1899 a letter to Meynell refers to the Christmas visit of Anselm and another friar:

I should be dead indeed to all that is beautiful in life if I failed to see how deliberately you set about making our stay at Palace Court the pleasure to us which you intended it to be. The tableaux, the unseen singer of the Gregorian notes of Christian dignity, Alice's incomparable rendering of the Adeste, the corybantic children—and (a whisper comes deep from beneath the folds of Umbrian peasant's garb) Habana fragrance, the nectar of the gods, & the birds of the forest—ah! delicious memories all. Dear faithful friend.

Thompson was as much at home among such men—and with their austerities—as a man born to be solitary could be, and when Meynell judged him to be doing badly in London he went to

Crawley occasionally. The panacea of change of environment could not be neglected in the grim opium-struggle that was still going on—and it was a remedy that needed renewing. Meynell had never the opportunity himself to leave London; he was at this time having to make the hardest efforts of his existence in order to make both ends meet; the pressure of work was telling on his robust constitution, and this is the only time in his prime of life when letters from his friends are full of concern for his unwellness and his need to work when in that condition. Such letters reflect too the illnesses and accidents attendant on a large young family. The added anxiety of his responsibility for Thompson, when London in its turn seemed no longer the right place, made him turn thankfully to the Capuchins. Thompson was not everybody's guest. He went to Pantasaph in 1892. He was to be away from the drug-taking associations of London—and was to write. The first report came cheeringly from Father Marianus: "Thompson is ever so much better. He looks it too. He is less melancholy, in fact at times quite lively." And Thompson himself wrote:

C'en est fait, as regards the opium; though I have only just taken the turning which leads out of the debility consequent on ye breaking-off. But I am now able to begin to get about a bit, & take exercise. That is to say, I should be able but—which, next to my wish to tell you that I was safely out of ye opium, is ye motive of my writing. I can't get outdoors because snow has fallen, & by a foolish trick before I left London I have ruined my boots. Cowering over ye fire at Fernhead Road one night, I let my boot hang too near the bars; & before I noticed it, ye tip was burned off. The upper leather has come away from the sole, leaving the snow free to get in. So that just when I want & long for walking to act as a tonic against my debility, I am compelled to stay in the house. For the snow here is not like London snow, which I cannot face; it is virgin, dry and pleasant for walking, while ye air is sunny & clear. I am very comfortable, thanks to your kindness & forethought. Father Anselm seems to have taken a fancy to me—also he is afraid of my being lonely—& comes to see me every other day. He took me all over ye monastery on Monday,

42

& has just left me after a prolonged discussion of the things which "none of us know anything about," as Marianus says when he is getting the worst of an argument.

This move to Pantasaph in fact took on a nature of permanence; he was still there four years later, though there were long visits at intervals to Palace Court. He stayed at first in Bishop's House at the monastery gate; later he lodged at the village post office, and, last, in a cottage on the hill behind the monastery. It is from Pantasaph that a great proportion of his letters to his friend were written; this was their longest time apart. And though Pantasaph, like indeed any other place, could not be consistently successful, he did during his time there in the keen mountain air acquire an appearance of well-being never seen by those who knew him only later—as is shown in the photograph taken in 1894.

But while the poet himself went to this Welsh retreat, his poetry was to come into the open. The firm of Elkin Mathews and John Lane was producing in 1893 a book of essays and one of poems by Alice Meynell. There were now negotiations for Thompson's poems to be issued by the same publishers in the same year. To Wilfrid Meynell it was like the launching of a battleship, as crucial and seeming-precarious; he believed it was a great poet who was to see the light—but with the trepidation of a personal belief in the almost impossible. Having already dexterously sewn Thompson's poems together, he was now in treaty for a volume to go further. Such fostering was to be a lifelong task. At the service of many other writers his function of a go-between was often in use: an early instance is shown in the voluminous letters to him from the poet Aubrey de Vere who, in difficulties with publishers, found that the energy and resource of his young friend as adviser and negotiator were tirelessly at his service. Meynell was often the practical man set among those wanting that quality.

In the present case there was of course no smooth path with Thompson:

I find Lane has already announced ye poems in his book list, so I am bound to go through with them; else I would let them go to the devil. I made myself ill with overstudy, & have been obliged to give my head three weeks' entire rest. But I am much better again now. Inwardly I suffer like old Nick; but ye blessed mountain air keeps up my body, & for ye rest— my Lady Pain and I are *au mieux*. . . . The country here is just beginning to get beautiful, & I am feeling ye first quickening pulse of spring. Lord, it is good for me to be here—very good. The clogged wheels in me are slowly beginning to move.

There was a question of the dedication verse.

I cannot consent [Thompson wrote to Meynell] to ye withdrawal of *your* name. You have of course ye right to refuse to accept ye dedication to yourself. But in that case I have ye right to withdraw ye dedication altogether, as I should certainly do. I should belie ye truth & my own feelings if I represented Mrs. Meynell as ye sole person to whom I owe what it has been given to me to accomplish in poetry. Suffer this—the sole thing . . . which links this first, possibly this only volume, with your name—suffer this to stand. I will feel deeply hurt if you refuse me this gratification.

So "To Wilfrid and Alice Meynell" headed the lines:

> If the rose in meek duty
> May dedicate humbly
> To her grower the beauty
> Wherewith she is comely;
> If the mine to the miner
> The jewels that pined in it,
> Earth to diviner
> The springs he divined in it;
> To the grapes the wine-pitcher
> Their juice that was crushed in it,
> Viol to its witcher
> The music lay hushed in it;
> If the lips may pay Gladness
> In laughters she wakened,
> And the heart to its sadness
> Weeping unslakened,

If the hid and sealed coffer,
　Whose having not his is,
To the loosers may proffer
　Their findings—here this is;
Their lives, if all livers
　To the Life of all living,
To you, O dear givers!
　I give your own giving.

There were other small animated points of dissension as the proof-sheets passed and repassed between Palace Court and Pantasaph. He had the right to the last word. "I send you ye line altered altogether. This must do. The stanza cannot go out." "I have received the finding of the Court Martial over which you presided; to which the undersigned begs to make answer," etc.

As for "immediatably" it is in all respects ye one & only right word for the line, as regards ye exact shade of meaning & feeling, & as regards ye rhythmical movement it gives to ye line. So it must absolutely & without any question stand— woe's me for ye public! But indeed, what is ye public doing *dans cette galere?* I believe, it is true, ye public has an odd kind of prejudice that poems are written for its benefit. It might as well suppose that when a woman loves, she bears children for its benefit; or (in ye case of ye poem in question) that when a man is hurt, he bleeds for its benefit.

Alice Meynell wrote: "Here are your wonderful poems— most wonderful and beautiful. It is a great event to me to send you these proofs." He wrote:

I need hardly say how grateful I was to receive a letter from you. I return herewith ye pages. . . . It seems to me that they read better than I had expected—particularly ye large additions to "To A Poet Breaking Silence," which were written at a time when I was by no means very fit for poetry, and so caused me some anxiety. . . . Your interest in ye volume is very dear to me. I cannot say I myself feel any elation about it. I am past the time when such things brought me any elation.

45

V

WHEN *Poems* appeared, however, he was not indifferent. It would have been difficult to maintain that mood in face of the communications fired at him by his friend in his own enthusiasm. In Meynell it was always a ready instinct to get a line of good tidings or encouragement into an envelope to someone and just catch the post with it; and, bent over his sea of papers, to forward a review or a letter giving some outside opinion was the work of a moment—when so near at hand lay the pen with its ink still wet from the moment before. He could crowd a remarkable amount into a brief time. It was a long habit—doing at speed the thing which was received somewhere in a leisure of enjoyment. It would almost seem as if six o'clock delayed a few moments for him—while one of his children stood by ready to rush to the pillar-box. The sign to some absent person was as necessary as to send the printer his material. It was not that he studied politeness, but a facet of the fact that it was on affection that his character was founded. A chance phrase in a letter to him from his wife when she was staying with her sister Elizabeth (Mimi) Butler remarks on this: "Many thanks for sending the telegram to Mimi. You are so good in telegrams and letters; no one else does things with so nice a grace."

The book was beautifully produced by Lane and had a frontispiece by Laurence Housman. When poetry has fallen into its place with time, it is difficult to recover the critical attitude of suspicion before it and the world have grown older together. What confronted the critics from the man they had never heard of? No lyric stintedness, but poetry full-blown in its size and images as if it presumed to the style and abundance of the great established poets. There was "A Fallen Yew"—the yew made it would seem to "un-edge the scythe of Time."

It seemed corrival of the world's great prime,
　　Made to un-edge the scythe of Time,
　　　And last with stateliest rhyme. . . .

When doom puffed out the stars, we might have said,
　　It would decline its heavy head,
　　　And see the world to bed.

For this firm yew did from the vassal leas,
　　And rain and air, its tributaries,
　　　Its revenue increase,

And levy impost on the golden sun,
　　Take the blind years as they might run,
　　　And no fate seek or shun.

But now our yew is strook, is fallen—yea
　　Hacked like dull wood of every day
　　　To this and that, men say.

Never!—To Hades' shadowy shipyards gone,
　　Dim barge of Dis, down Acheron
　　　It drops, or Lethe wan. . . .

There was "The Hound of Heaven." There were also lines
of autobiographical suffering to be distinguished from their
setting:

　　　　　Life is a coquetry
　　　　　Of Death, which wearies me,
　　　　　　　Too sure
　　　　　　　Of the amour.

　　　　　A tiring-room where I
　　　　　Death's divers garments try,
　　　　　　　Till fit
　　　　　　　Some fashion sit.

　　　　　It seemeth me too much
　　　　　I do rehearse for such
　　　　　　　A mean
　　　　　　　And simple scene.

47

The sandy glass hence bear—
Antique remembrancer;
My veins
Do spare its pains . . .

The longest poem was "Love in Dian's Lap," a sequence of the poems inspired by Alice Meynell since he had first known her. He was enthralled by her mind—even by her mere knowledge. "I wonder what she does not know," he had unburdened himself to the family friend to whom he occasionally wrote.

A mistress of poetry, an exquisite art-critic, she knows, besides, music, Latin, Greek, Italian, French, German, & all kinds of multifarious things at which I can but dimly guess.

He was moved by her delicacy and continued:

Her soul has indeed "fretted ye pigmy body to decay," but fragile she must always have been. Her youthful portraits show a beautiful, spiritualised face, with musing, saddened eyes; ye head, in most portraits, drooped as with ye weight of thought. Yet ye mournful sweetness of ye countenance is preserved from anything merely weak & poetessish by its contained quiet. A face which is a poem as beautiful as any she has written.

But this was a selfless observer, the most detached human being whom those who knew him could well conceive of. A love of his could not even be a hopeless love—too unhoping for that, too remote from life's actual circumstances. In a room he was only half a presence, there and not there, for even if he should be tediously harping on some minor lateness or mislaying, it was with the strange ineffective gentleness of one whose stream of life is elsewhere. So also his love of Alice Meynell, except in some rare moment of tension, was absent even from the very room in which he and his friends worked together, and flowed only into his poetry.

How should I gauge what beauty is her dole,
Who cannot see her countenance for her soul;
As birds see not the casement for the sky?
And as 'tis check they prove its presence by,
I know not of her body till I find
My flight debarred the heaven of her mind.

48

Hers is the face whence all should copied be,
Did God make replicas of such as she:
Its presence felt by what it does abate,
Because the soul shines through tempered and mitigate . . .
There amorous Thought has sucked pale Fancy's breath,
And Tenderness sits looking toward the lands of death;
There Feeling stills her breathing with her hand,
And Dream from Melancholy part wrests the wand;
And on this lady's heart, looked you so deep,
Poor Poetry has rocked himself to sleep:
Upon the heavy blossom of her lips
Hangs the bee Musing; nigh her lids eclipse
Each half-occulted star beneath those eyes,
Passionless passion, wild tranquillities.

And when there is a lover's cry it is different from the cries of
other lovers.

Lady who hold'st on me dominion!
Within your spirit's arms I stay me fast
    Against the fell
Immitigate ravening of the gates of hell;
And claim my right in you, most hardly won,
Of chaste fidelity upon the chaste:
Hold me and hold by me, lest both should fall
(O in high escalade high companion!)
Even in the breach of Heaven's assaulted wall.
Like to a wind-blown sapling grow I from
The clift, Sweet, of your skyward-jetting soul,—
Shook by all gusts that sweep it, overcome
By all its clouds incumbent: O be true
To your soul, dearest, as my life to you!
For if that soil grow sterile, then the whole
Of me must shrivel, from the topmost shoot
Of climbing poesy, and my life, killed through,
Dry down and perish to the foodless root.

But what his readers had to take from him too was the verbal
exuberance which the starved years had somehow fed in him—
riotous lines, the strange fruit of the meagre existence—making

his friends at Palace Court warn him that the meaning was sometimes lost in the "foam and roar of your phraseology." *Poems* was not innocent of this defect, which was to increase. This is the beginning of "A Corymbus for Autumn."

Hearken my chant, 'tis
As a Bacchante's,
A grape-spurt, a vine-splash, a tossed tress, flown vaunt 'tis!
Suffer my singing,
Gipsy of Seasons, ere thou go winging;
Ere Winter throws
His slaking snows
In thy feasting-flagon's impurpurate glows!
The sopped sun—toper as ever drank hard—
Stares foolish, hazed,
Rubicund, dazed,
Totty with thine October tankard.

(But J. L. Garvin said of this poem: "To be familiar with it is to repent of having ever reproached it for a splendid pedantry and a monstrous ambition.") Thompson got a mixed reception for *Poems*, with enough good to put against much bad. The *Westminster Gazette* critic said of one poem: "Is it poetry? is it sense? is it English?" Another: "His faults are fundamental." And H. D. Traill wrote to Meynell: "A 'public' to appreciate 'The Hound of Heaven' is to me inconceivable." Of two fellow poets, Le Gallienne was enthusiastic, for he had been John Lane's reader whose report began: "Would certainly publish"; the other, John Davidson, wrote: "Here are dominion—domination of language, and a sincerity as of Robert Burns." Arthur Symons was coldly, doubtfully, appreciative. And Clement Shorter called him "the poet of a small Catholic clique"—starting something which flourished when *Sister Songs* was published two years later, when a critic was "sorry for Mr. Thompson to think that he had been spoiled by indiscreet flatterers," and another leading one referred to "the frenzied paeans of his admirers by profession."

But *Poems* had kinder treatment from the critics than Thompson's two later volumes were going to have. His reactions came to Meynell.

Will it be believed, however, that after deprecating superlatives I am actually disposed to rank myself higher than Mr. Le Gallienne's final sentence might seem to imply? I absolutely think my poetry "greater" than any work by a *new* poet which has appeared since Rossetti. Unless, indeed, ye greater work to which ye critic referred was Mrs. Meynell's. I frankly admit that her poetry has exquisite unclamorous qualities beside which all ye fireworks of my own work are much less enduring things. Otherwise, I will not vail my crest to Henley, or Robert Bridges, or even William Watson. . . . I am very pleased with all the letters you have sent me. . . .

I have read in ye *Register* with great surprise that ye *Poems* are exhausted. I am even more glad for my publisher's sake than for my own; since, to tell you the truth, I have been haunted by ye fear that Lane's generosity had led him to expend more on ye book than he would succeed in recouping. . . . The *St. James's* article I am very pleased with. I only deprecate in it the implied comparison to Dante, and the to me bewildering comparison to Matthew Arnold. It is not merely that I have studied no poet less; it is that I should have thought we were in ye sharpest contrast. His characteristic fineness lies in that very form and restraint to which I so seldom attain: his characteristic drawback in ye lack of that full stream which I am seldom without. The one needs and becomes strict banks—for he could not fill wider ones: ye other too readily overflows all banks.

Such serene letters were not always forthcoming from Pantasaph. Mrs. Blackburn, who was now at Pantasaph, wrote to the Meynells:

As for Francis—I hardly know what to say. I gave him all your messages and I wish he would show some kind of human elation at his unprecedented success, but he seems to take it all in a dull mechanical sort of way which is distressing. It is two months now since there has been a change in him. I feel he is some way or other getting into the old habit and a fortnight ago I spoke to him about it, for not I alone had noticed the change but others also. However, he has assured Father Anselm solemnly that he is not taking opium, but he is certainly taking something. I am advised not to say anything more to him so I try to make him as cheerful as is possible, but he stays away for days together, and although he has promised to come up for tea this afternoon ten to one I shan't see him. . . . It is so odd to read all the well-merited praise and then realize how outside the pale of humanity this genius is, more irresponsible than any child, with a child's fits of temper and want of foresight and control. . . . He isn't doing a stroke of work and stops in bed the best part of the day, and lately he falls asleep when he comes to see me in the way he used to do at Palace Court.

In the beginning of 1894, therefore, Wilfrid and Alice Meynell went for a few days to Pantasaph. In recording her impression of the half-mined, half-cultivated country with the monastic group of buildings high in a cleft among the hills Alice Meynell wrote: "The poet lives at the monastery gates, and on monastery ground, in a seclusion which the tidings of the sequence of his editions hardly reaches. There is no disturbing renown to be got among the cabins of the Flintshire hills. Homeward, over the verge, from other valleys, his light figure flits at nightfall, like a moth."

Dearest Wilfrid & Alice,

As you are together in my thoughts let me join you together in this note. I cannot express to you what deep happiness your visit gave me; how dear it was to see your faces again. I think "ye leaves fell from the day" indeed when your train went out of ye station; & I never heard ye birds with such sad voices. . . .

Yours ever,
Francis Thompson

And Mrs. Blackburn wrote: "No one sees him but Fr. Anselm, to whom he comes every evening and whom he tells of his work. He told him last night that since you left he seemed to have a return of all the old poetical power. Of course he is flying over hill and dale and never to be seen, but I am sure you will be as glad as I am at this fresh development—especially as your and Alice's visit has evidently called it forth."

Thompson himself wrote again:

I accidentally sat up all last night, & did not discover ye fact until day came through ye blind. Consequently I am suffering for it today. As for poetry—I am despondent when I am without a poetical fit, yet when I have one I am miserable on account of my prose. I came lately across a letter of Keats' (penned in ye prae-Endymion days) which might almost word for word be written by myself about myself. It expresses exactly one of ye things which trouble me, & make me sometimes despair of my career. "I find [he says] I cannot do without poetry—without eternal poetry; half ye day will not do—the whole of it. I began with a little, but habit has made me a leviathan. I had become all in a tremble from not having written anything of late: ye Sonnet overleaf did me good; I slept ye better last night for it; this morning, however, I am nearly as bad again." I, too, have been "all in a tremble" because I had written nothing of late. I am constantly expecting to wake up some morning & find that my Daemon has abandoned me. I hardly think I *could* be very vain of my literary gift; for I so keenly feel that it is beyond my power to command, & may at any moment be taken from me.

The poems he was writing were those which accumulated till their publication in 1897. For *Sister Songs*, published now in 1895, had been written more or less contemporaneously with *Poems*. It is a long poem-sequence in two parts, "An Offering to Two Sisters, Monica and Madeline [Sylvia]," the Meynells' daughters. His original title for the poem was "Amphicypellon." He wrote to Meynell:

When Schliemann's things from Troy were first exhibited at South Kensington, I remember seeing among them a drinking-cup labelled "Perhaps the *amphicypellon* of Homer." It was a boat-shaped cup of plain gold, open at the top and with a crescentic aperture at either extremity of the rim, through which the wine could be either poured or drunk. So that you could pour from either end, & (if the cup were *brimmed* with wine) two people could have drunk from it at the same time, one at either extremity. In a certain sense, therefore, it was a double cup. And it had also two handles, one at either of its boat-shaped sides, so that it was a two-handled cup. You will see at once why I have applied the name to my double poem. . . . Let it be "Sister Songs" as you suggest. But keep "an offering to two sisters" where it is now—on the title page.

Though he had originally thought this poem unworthy of publication, it was launched eventually with less trepidation than the first book. "I shall be disappointed if my new volume does not make a success," he wrote. "I have great hopes when I look at the poems as a collection." But later he had to speak of "my ill-starred volume—which has sold only 349 copies in twelve months." It is a rhymed poem, in varied metre, in parts a "dance of words," in others grim with his own experiences. It was less well received generally and sold less than the former book. E. K. Chambers expressed a common exasperation. "He showers out obsolete words, or at will coins new ones, with a profusion that at times becomes extravagant and grotesque. . . . His freaks of speech rarely prove anything but ugly linguistic monstrosities." From an unexpected quarter came something very different— Arnold Bennett in *Woman*:

I declare that for three days after this book appeared I read nothing else. I went about repeating snatches of it. My belief is that Francis Thompson has a richer natural genius, a finer poetical equipment, than any poet save Shakespeare. Show me the divinest glories of Shelley and Keats, even of the Tennyson who wrote the "Lotus Eaters" and the songs in "The Princess," and I think I can match them all out of this one book, this little book that can be bought at an ordinary bookseller's shop for an ordinary, prosaic crown. I fear that in thus extolling Francis Thompson's work, I am grossly outraging the canons of criticism. For the man is alive, he gets up of a morning like common mortals, not improbably he eats bacon for breakfast; and every critic with an atom of discretion knows that a poet must not be called great until he is either dead or very old. Well, please yourself what you think. But, in time to come, don't say I didn't tell you.

Mr. Garvin, for whom Thompson's poems had an enchantment since his first sight of one in *Merry England*, made a summing-up of his general verdict later, in 1897, in the *Bookman*, in the course of which he said:

> After the publication of his second volume, when it became clear that "The Hound of Heaven" and "Sister Songs" should be read together as a strict lyrical sequence, there was no longer any comparison possible except with the highest, the inevitable comparison with even Shakespeare's Sonnets. The Sonnets are the greatest soliloquy in literature. "The Hound of Heaven" and "Sister Songs" together are the second greatest; and there is no third. In each case it is rather consciousness imaged in the magic mirror of poetry than explicit autobiography.

Thompson had a certain amount of lodging-shifting in Pantasaph at this time.

> I write to relieve your perplexities. I can obtain lodgings on the same terms as at present, with the people that used to have me before I went to Ivy Cottage. Consequently you need not be called on for pre-payment. . . . I shall be with people that I know and like, and who know and like me, and will not want to get rid of me on account of my erratic ways. They are used to them of old, and like me well enough not to mind them.

The lodging was at Creccas Cottage. A receipt for payment reads: "Boarding weekly at 15 Shillings per week for 12 weeks £9. Washing 6 Shillings. Due the 6 of March. Received March 10 with thanks." He had entered on the last year of the Pantasaph sojourn, and in April his father died aged seventy-two. Thompson went to Ashton but not in time to see his father alive.

Creccas Cottage, Pantasaph.
May 2nd/96.

Dear Wilfrid,
I shall be forwarding my book in a few days, when I will answer Mrs. Meynell's letter; for ye kindness and sympathy

55

of which, in ye meantime, I thank her warmly. I enclose herewith my landlady's bill. Also Fr. Sebastian advanced me a sovereign for my journey to Ashton, which I must ask you to repay him. As I managed to lose ye return half of my ticket, and had to get another, it did not more than carry me through, with my expenses at ye other end. Likewise I had to get a new pair of boots to go in, ye ones I had being quite impossible; but though I forward you ye bill for these, I should hope this latter item may be able to stand over for a while, unlike the other two.

I never saw my father again. I cannot speak about it at present. . . . It has been nothing but ill-health and sorrow lately—but I must not trouble you with these things.

I saw my sister, looking the merest girl still, and sweeter than ever. She did not look a day older than ten years ago. She said I looked very changed and worn, older than my portrait. Everybody made ye same flattering remark.

I hear that there is an article concerning me in ye *Edinburgh Review*. I should be very glad if you will—or can—send me ye *Edinburgh*. It would do me good; I never since I knew you felt so low-hearted and empty of all belief in myself. I could find it in my heart to pitch my book into ye fire; and I shall be thoroughly glad to get it off to you, for my heart sinks at ye sight or thought of it. The one remaining poem which had stuck in my gizzard at ye last I succeeded in polishing off last night, sitting up all night to do it; and I must start on ye Preface as soon as this letter is off. . . .

Yours always,
Francis Thompson

The book of which he was sending the MS. was *New Poems*, his last. There was a question of a change of publisher.

. . . Moreover I think Lane would want ye book cut down. Now, if Alice & you, *after you have read it in proof*, say "this is bad poetry," I will cut out half the book; but not half a line to please a publisher's whim for little books and big margins. I was cabinned & confined over my first book; with my spurs won, I should be at liberty to make this book comprehensive.

WILFRID MEYNELL

as a young man

ALICE MEYNELL
about the time of her marriage

... I believe this will be my last volume of poetry—in any case my last for some years—and I am determined to make it complete, that I may feel all my work worth anything is on record for posterity, if I die. ... It is my poetic last will and testament; I have been preparing it for three years, and I will not make it less complete for mere publisher's reasons.

I must ask you and Alice to defer your reading of it till you have it in proof. It is utterly strange to you, will need judging from other standpoints than my work you are used to; you will perhaps think well to recommend important omissions: and such recommendations would carry no weight if you had read it in Ms. After you have read it in proof, they would have my attentive ear, so long as they are based purely on defect of poetry. You have often recast a judgment made on my Ms.; not often, I think, after you had seen my work in print. ... I have gained, I think, in art and chastity of style; but have greatly lost in fire and glow. It is time that I was silent. This book carries me quite as far as my dwindling strength will allow; and if I wrote further in poetry, I should write down my own fame.

The lighter kind of request to his friend was: "May I remind you that I am owing poor Fr. Raphael some tobacco; also that sonnets & suchlike commodities will by no means flow without smoke." "Will you kindly send me a few stamps. I get my supplies from Anselm without difficulty; but since he is away I notice that ye authorities begin to look black when I have to ask them to stamp several letters in succession." And then came the December of 1896. "Let it be Wednesday, as you suggest. I trust to you to send me my fare in time"—and the long productive time at Pantasaph was at an end.

VI

THE Meynells' friends were literary ones, such as the occasions of their exclusively literary life brought them.

An early one of these was a man whose name was a poem in itself, or at least his poet friends could not help turning it into one. Walter Savage Landor had once greeted him: "Make thy proud name still prouder for thy sons, Aubrey de Vere!" And his friend Tennyson used the names of Lady de Vere and even Vere de Vere straight out of the family. Sir Henry Taylor wrote in a tribute to this gentle idealist:

> No lesser light
> Than what was lit in Sydney's spirit clear,
> Or given to saintly Herbert's to diffuse,
> Now lives in thine, de Vere.

And "To Aubrey de Vere Esquire" looked well heading a sonnet by William Watson.

Aubrey de Vere knew Wilfrid Meynell and Alice Thompson independently of each other before their marriage. In 1876 he wrote to Meynell:

> Curragh Chase, Adare.
> Easter Monday, 1876.

My dear Sir,

Pray accept my best thanks for your very kind letter, which reminded me pleasantly of that delightful day I spent at St. Etheldreda's last summer when I saw those memorable walls which so strangely and delightfully blended one's recollection of the Catholic Past with one's hopes for the Catholic future. I must also ask you to accept my thanks for the very beautiful Sonnet which you have connected with my name. Your lines give me far more than my due; but they are among those things which make me hope that my poetry, which has met with little circulation, may yet do some good one day, or give a pleasure which is not wholly an idle pleasure. I was particularly pleased by your alluding in your Sonnet to my father's poetry. It has hitherto not met the fame it well deserves. His "Mary Tudor" has only this year become known. His Sonnets show that he possessed the meditative vein as well as the impassioned and dramatic—a union very rare. He would have felt as I do that there is no higher or truer poetry to be found than in holy labours such as those in which your little community at St. Etheldreda's are daily employed. Pray present my kindest remembrances to Father Lockhart and believe me very sincerely yours,

Aubrey de Vere

And in that same year he was addressing "Dear Miss Thompson" about her poetry. "You take suggestions as well as Henry Taylor does but you must remember also the bargain that he and I have always made, viz. that the Author must be really the best judge. . . . Correcting is a great art. Campbell used to correct his poetry into confusion, and sometimes left out his best lines." And in another letter reproaching her for her "elisions":

> To show that I am not altogether a bigot I will give you carte blanche for any number of such elisions as you find in the first 26 lines of Paradise Lost, nearly all of which are either elisions to the eye not ear, or else affect the ear only as the palate of the gourmand was affected when he made his cook rub an onion to the *outside* of the dish in which he sent up his beefsteak. . . . We must not, to be revenged on Pope, who mistook mellifluousness for Harmony, forget that there is a noble as well as an ignoble smoothness, that such smoothness is a part of Majesty, not of daintiness or prettiness, and that Poetry will not dispense with it except in her "reserved cases."

He then heard of their approaching marriage.

Curragh Chase, Adare.
Jan. 16, 1877.

My dear Miss Thompson,

You send me great news: and I cannot let a moment pass without telling you how ardently I hope that your marriage may prove rich in all the best and truest happiness that this earth can know. Other happiness you would not value. I am very glad that your future Husband is one whom I already know, and of whom I know so much that is good, not only as regards matters of literature but as regards still higher things. After having shared the holy labours of the Brothers of Charity, in whose house I first met him, it is but just that he should have a happy home of his own. Remember that no other tie is to relax your first bond—your engagement to *Poetry*. Otherwise we Poets shall have to write Satires on Marriage.

Yours ever sincerely,
Aubrey de Vere

Later he introduced the young couple to Sir Percy and Lady Shelley at Bournemouth in order that they might see Shelley relics, and Meynell had the strange experience of hearing a portly middle-aged man refer to the immortal youth as "my poor father." He introduced them also to Sir Henry Taylor, of *Philip van Artevelde* fame, and his wife—and was perhaps a little relieved that his young protégés made a good impression. "I must just send you a line to assure you that if you found pleasure in his society, he and Lady Taylor found pleasure no less in yours and your Husband's, and are quite looking forward to renewing so pleasant an acquaintance. You must therefore take care to call on them whenever you are near them again." Aubrey de Vere was godfather to Monica, the Meynells' second child.

His poems and dramas ran to many volumes; he described his aim as "the promotion of a taste for imaginative literature in the Catholic Body." He gradually came to consult Meynell on all the moves in his somewhat abortive literary career. He was a Wordsworth worshipper, and wrote articles on him. "I hardly know whether or not it would be lawful and right to put an Essay on such a subject into the 19*th Cent.*, which inserts also Infidel Essays, though excellent men have thought it right to publish papers antagonistic to those Infidel ones in that Journal. I have myself published letters in *The Times*, which has often attacked

Ireland most unjustly as well as when her sons have deserved it, and is always misrepresenting the Church." The letters indeed which he wrote to Meynell during a long friendship would fill a volume, but it would be one mostly of anxious questionings concerning publishers and printers and periodicals, and above all the —for him—vital question of the insurance of books. For it was hard that within the space of a few years two fires at his publisher's destroyed the stocks of most of his books. The complications concerning author's *versus* publisher's insurance: the questions of compensation arising in the case of volumes published on commission; the alternative for insurance-payments as between commercial value or cost of re-publication, and as between "moral rights and legal claims"—all these made an imbroglio out of which the bewildered poet could only pray at great length to be extricated by sound knowledgeable advice; anything he himself could find out he reported to Meynell as chief diplomat. "Now two Publishers, Oates, and Bell (C. Patmore's Publishers) say that Insurance does not mean 'Commercial Value' but does mean the repayment to the Author of the whole sum necessary to replace the lost vols—paper, printing and binding. I wrote to five Insurance Offices. Three of them made the same statement as those two Publishers, the other two seem to assert Kegan Paul & Co.'s principle of *Commercial Value*." He had supreme confidence in the business-acumen of his young friend. "Lord Tennyson and Canon Ainger think that I ought to accept Arnold's proposal," he wrote in regard to his *Recollections*. But Meynell had to decide. In 1895 de Vere wrote with a shaky hand: "Our meeting the other evening was like the old times, which become more to us as the end draws nearer, and the Past recedes." He met Thompson at Palace Court. The difference in their generations was hard to span. His only reference to the younger poet in his letters was— rather as one determined not to see for himself: "What is Mr. Thompson's new book of poems like?" He was a stately, lovable, upright man. Meynell had occasion to write reminiscently of him when reviewing in the *Observer* in 1925 *Guests and Memories,* written by Sir Henry Taylor's daughter Una—as follows:

61

Closest among the close friends of the Taylors at Bournemouth was Aubrey de Vere. I quote from memory the story, not repeated in these pages, of the visit Aubrey once paid to his beloved Sir William Rowan Hamilton, whose little boy, when chided for not recognising the visitor, said: "Thinking about God and thinking about Latin, I had forgotten Aubrey de Vere." But he was unforgettable by all adults who knew. him, a poet of almost supreme excellence in one sonnet ("For we the mighty mountain plains have trod"), and in his "Daffodil" and "Autumnal" Odes; a man of heroic fortitude and self-denial during the Irish Famine, that "Year of Sorrow" also nobly signalised in his song. He was a first-cousin of the hostess, in early life her adorer, in all his life her more than brother. Henry Taylor spoke of him as a saint—no; that was not quite adequate—as two saints! There was yet another relationship to life which his cousin desired for him after her first birth of a son: "I had great pity for you because you could never be a mother!" Every year of his mature life he came from his Irish home at Curragh Chase to Pall Mall and the Athenaeum for the summer season, and then left on a round of visits to The Roost, to Tennyson, to John Henry Newman. He was a sublime master-of-ceremonies, always introducing to each other men and women who might serve or delight each other in the mad dance of life. Just as he had first wrung from Wordsworth a recognition of the young Tennyson—"Yes, stately, stately"—so later he brought younger poets to the now happily ruling Tennyson for his benison. Guests at the Taylors walked out with him along the then little-frequented cliffs, and to them he recited Wordsworth in tones rumoured to reproduce Wordsworth's very own.

The friendship with the Taylors which he had provided for the Meynells was a pleasant one to them, and before the days of their numerous children they were free to pay visits to the Roost at Bournemouth. In 1880 Meynell had first made use of the name John Oldcastle in writing a small book called *Journals and Journalism*, which was something more than a text-book for young writers. Sir Henry Taylor, in his eighty-first year, wrote then, not knowing the identity of the author:

The Roost, Bournemouth.
16 May 1880.

Dear Mr. Oldcastle,

(If that is yr. name) I have just finished yr. book on Journals & Journalism & have acquired from it a large knowledge of the wonderful world of writing & publishing we live in, of which I had next to no knowledge before. Like so many of those of whom you write I began my literary life (if my life can be called literary) with an article in a Journal—on Moore in the Quarterly Review (Oct. 1822)—short, light & impertinent. In the next year or two I wrote two articles in the same Journal, & then, being greatly occupied with public business in the Colonial Office, I left off writing for the Press.

Before the last of my articles I had repented of the spirit in which the others had been written & on two or three occasions in after life when I have written articles I have not, I think, said anything by which anyone cd. be hurt or offended. I recognize in your book the charitable spirit which I shd. wish to see in the Press. I have sometimes been led to ask whether there is such a thing as a goodnatured newspaper. There are themes & occasions of course when we are to be "angry & sin not," & in reading your account of some journals the question occurred to me whether you are not too tolerant—but I know of them only by report & I may be mistaken. At all events yr. book is very interesting & here & there most amusing & I am much obliged to you for sending it.

Believe me, yours faithfully,
Henry Taylor

Taylor had already in 1875 taken an interest—somewhat carping, with a charge of obscurity—in Alice Thompson's *Preludes,* writing as a stranger to her: "And with regard to your versification, in that also I meet with difficulties, & I do not know whether what is peculiar is due to a theory of versification or to an idiosyncrasy of the ear. Tennyson, whose versification is one of the great charms of his work, in his latter utterances allowed theories to betray him into a line here & there which nothing but theory cd. dictate. I hope that in his forthcoming drama we shall find him 'Warbling his native woodnotes wild.'"

Meynell, having a slight acquaintance with Stevenson, who was going to Bournemouth for his health, asked the Taylors to see him. "I will ask him to come to luncheon on Sunday," Lady Taylor replied. "I have heard from my nephew, Stephen Spring-Rice, that he is a most agreeable person."

Stevenson wrote to Meynell:

> Skerryvore, Alum Chine Road, Bournemouth.
> 21st May 1885.
>
> My dear Sir,
>
> I remember very well meeting you one famous afternoon at the Savile, and learning, only after you were gone, that you were the husband of a poetess whose verses I had often admired. I have now to thank you for your introduction to the Taylors. I have seen as yet only the young ladies, with whom we are much delighted; but I soon hope to make out a visit myself. The notice in the *Weekly Register* (so long unacknowledged) was to me of a very high interest; its setting perhaps more so than itself; above all the pathetic tale of Gordon and Newman.[1] How one envied the Cardinal! And yet I know too little of the opinions of the Church to know if his feelings wd. not be more painful than agreeable. With many thanks, believe me very truly yours,
>
> Robert Louis Stevenson

To the Meynells the Taylors were always a revered remembrance—she with her beauty and what Stevenson was to call "her high mind and her hot impatient heart"; and he with his noble presence. (It was said: "Something in him corresponded to the greatest beard of his age.") When they died their two daughters carried on the friendship, and even linked those somehow illustrious days with the Francis Thompson days, during which Ida Taylor wrote to Meynell: "Mr. Lane Fox was here yesterday and speaking about Mr. Francis Thompson. He is very anxious to meet you and to tell you of an exhaustive study he has lately been making, under a doctor, of hypnotism and its results in

[1] *The Dream of Gerontius*, with passages about death heavily underlined, was in Gordon's possession when he died.

64

HENRY EDWARD CARDINAL MANNING

curing those who have become opium-eaters. I promised to ask you to meet him."

In considering Meynell's main friends the common denominator to be seen among them is that they were men of strong independent views, not afraid to be the exception. It is possible to think of the names of many with whom he had much in common and with whom acquaintance never went far if they were without the unconvention-quality of his own leanings. To be in a minority was after all the English climate for a Catholic, and one which must have suited him well enough since his affinity was with the anti-imperialists, Home Rulers, Boer War dissentients, and extreme social reformers. The man who in most of these respects qualified for his hero was Manning, a Cardinal who, Meynell said, "fluttered a red robe in the face of John Bull," whose abiding concern was the rights of Labour and conditions of the poor, who as a temperance reformer of extreme personal asceticism said: "If I were an Irish hodman I would be a drunkard," and who described Dickens to his Seminarians as "a complete course of moral theology." It was exactly what many would think outrageous in the Cardinal's remarks to him that Meynell treasured and told all his life; his saying of certain co-religionists: "I have always known they were good Catholics; perhaps one day they may be good Christians." "Do you know that the Jews are taking better care of their working girls in the East End than we are? What are our people doing? Oh, I forgot, they are examining their consciences." "We are putting up statues to saints instead of being them." Writing to his small schoolboy son Meynell quoted Manning's "If we only knew how ready God is to forgive us we should never offend him."

In 1884 Meynell was able to effect an interesting introduction. He had made the acquaintance of Henry George, and it seemed as if of all men Manning was the one Henry George should meet —Manning who had written of land-owning in Ireland:

There is a natural and divine law, anterior and superior to all human and civil law, by which every people has a right to live of the fruits of the soil on which they are born, and in

65

WILFRID SCAWEN BLUNT, about 1900

which they are buried. The Land Question, as we call it by a somewhat heartless euphemism, means hunger, thirst, nakedness, notice to quit, labour spent in vain, the toil of years seized upon, the breaking up of homes, the miseries, sicknesses, deaths, of parents, children, wives; the despair and wildness which spring up in the hearts of the poor when legal force, like a sharp harrow, goes over the most sensitive and vital rights of mankind. All this is contained in the Land Question.

The meeting Meynell brought about between two kindred thinkers is mentioned in Henry George's *Life* by his son.[1]

Purcell's *Life* of Manning when it came was a tribulation to Meynell, an "act of biographical brigandage," he called it, and saw in it the denigration of the Cardinal, "a process begun clumsily by Purcell and carried to artistic perfection by Strachey, a malformation by omission in which his closest friends could not recognize him."

In 1880 Manning, dissatisfied with the then policy of *The Tablet*, had purchased the *Weekly Register* in order to have his own views represented in a Catholic weekly. (Bishop Vaughan, owner of *The Tablet*, made anxious play with the fact to Manning: "With the best wishes not to injure *The Tablet*, you will not be able to help doing so. You are running a passenger boat for nothing on the Mississippi in order to beat and ruin an established company. With your Eminence as known proprietor it would be: 'The President of the U.S. aboard our boat!' ") In 1881 Manning sought a new editor for the paper, and on Lockhart's recommendation he made Meynell both editor and proprietor. He wrote to

[1] From the *Life of Henry George* by his son Henry George, Jr., 1900: "Although the several months in Great Britain had been, as a whole, strenuous, there were intervals of relaxation. One of these was when Wilfrid Meynell, editor of the Catholic *Weekly Register*, took Mr. George to meet Cardinal Manning. Mr. Meynell said after the death of both men: 'It was my great privilege to introduce Henry George to Cardinal Manning. I have a vision of the two profiles facing each other in the growing dusk, and I recall the emotion of tone in which each man made frankly to the other a sort of profession of faith. They had travelled to the same goal from opposite directions. "I loved the people," said Henry George, "and that love brought me to Christ as their best friend and teacher." "And I," said the Cardinal, "loved Christ, and so learned to love the people for whom He died." '"

him: "If I were sixty-four I should continue the *Weekly Register*; but I am seventy-four; the anxiety for its conduct is too great." But for the next ten years he kept a very vigilant eye on it. "I have just run over your second number," he wrote, "and unless in my haste I have made 'sviste' it is thoroughly good. The article on Leo XIII is far better than mine. And yours on the future of the *Weekly Register* is all I could desire. Never sink below that level and never go over those lines. This number stands my three tests: Catholic, Pure, Kindly. Keep to this and God will bless you." There began a constant intercourse between the old man and the young, still formal in its intimacy, for Meynell has noted that whereas Manning "had the habit of looking with a keen yet composed observation into any stranger's face, in a manner significant of his close relation to his flock—to whom it seemed on their part that his sermons reached them as private exhortations from one who must know their mental experiences—yet, on the other hand, his private friendship was made grave by the gentle severity, the old age, the characteristic reserve of address, and the spiritual dignity." The letters of ten years all begin "My dear Mr. Meynell." There were constant summonses. "Come with the bats at your usual hour of night. I shall be in by 9 o'clock." "Come & give an account of yourself, that I may tie a hundredweight to the tail of your imagination." Meynell must have worn down the steps of Archbishop's House; there were many others to do so too, and he might be crowded out. "If you will come on Sunday I shall believe you have forgiven the Austrian Ambassador, & me." "I have just had a talk with the Tablet, & I should like to talk to the Weekly Register. Come tomorrow evening." Manning amused himself by exaggerating the competition between the two papers. "The Hated Rival had what I struck out of the W. Register. Be consoled,—I thought of you, but did not remember the existence of the Hated Rival." By way of relaxation he wrote in 1882: "Will you come tomorrow at $\frac{1}{4}$ to 6, have tea, & go with me & Fr. Lockhart to see the Electric Light at the Chrystal Palace." Scoldings were not lacking. "Is not the naming of private persons a part of the society-style which you

67

so well denounced last week?" And: "You made a slip of the pen in the word separation [relating to Home Rule], & a slip of prudence in bringing in any reference to the Irish question for Children. But it will die, & die sooner if you are silent. No, a slip does not make me regret my Godfathership. But do not slip again."

On his side Meynell badgered him to write for his godchild, the paper (he was also godfather to the Meynells' second son), and for *Merry England* too. "Your tyranny is truly Arabian; I am fully dissatisfied with what I made under the last," wrote the Cardinal. And: "You slay first & rue afterwards—like Rhadamanthus. I hoped that an Olive Branch would turn away wrath. But you are a 'genus irritabile.'" Meynell was very conscious of the kindness which did not permit the plea "I have not time," and announced that in his editorial experience there was only one class of the community capable of exercising such kindness—the class of Cardinal Archbishops! With one of his contributions Manning wrote: "I am ashamed of myself but the inclosed may go, & if your readers only laugh at me it will make Merry England merrier." A summons towards the close of his life said: "Come for a minute. I want you to do what I think you will do willingly." This was a request to Meynell to befriend a woman who was likely to be despised as a party in a *cause célèbre*; he knew that no man could be more fitted to the humane part assigned to him.

The last call to Archbishop's House was an unspoken and unwritten one. It was in the January of 1892, and it was the Cardinal's illness that kept Meynell hovering at the doors when, he wrote, "the beautiful moon of that frosty night was all too surely to be the last of a holy and famous life."

He had of course been unable to forbear from bringing the Cardinal and Thompson together, and he turned to Thompson now for a poem on the dead man, and was well repaid, though rather than concentrating on its object it proved to be one of the most subjective of Thompson's poems. In a first version he begins by referring to the fact that he had gone but once to the

Cardinal's "stern bare home," and he claims his ear again now though dead.

> I saw thee only once,
> Although thy gentle tones
> Said soft
> "Come hither oft."

> Therefore my spirit clings
> Heaven's porter by the wings
> And holds
> Its gated golds

> Apart, with thee to press
> A private business;—
> Whence
> Deign me audience.

> Your singer did not come
> Back to that stern, bare home:
> He knew
> Himself and you.

> I saw, as seers do,
> That you were even you;
> And—why,
> I too was I. . . .

And he was here touching—as no one could do more convincedly —on the mutual inaccessibility of any one to any other.

It will be noticed that Manning did not use on Meynell the experienced, apt, discursive pen which made him in general so expressive a letter-writer—and this was not only because they were in frequent session. For the same thing applies to Meynell's other correspondents. They did not sharpen their brains for his benefit nor have to argue their cherished beliefs; it was for quick sympathy on the feeling-side of their lives, or for executive ability in any practical service needed that he was the person sought among many. And so it was with St. George Mivart.

Here again was a convert, and a man twenty-five years older than Meynell. A student of church architecture, Fellow of the Royal Society, secretary of the Linnaean Society, and author of the wide range of books suggested by a few of their titles—*Nature and Thought, Defence of Liberty of Conscience, The Myology of Certain Tailed Batrachians,* and *The Structure of the Fins of Fishes*—here also was another individualist, to the extent, indeed, eventually, of being charged with unorthodoxy. But he did not spend his plausible or convincing versatility in his letters to Meynell; he wrote mostly as one merely who would feel happier for the presence of his friend on a basis of mutual confidence and liking. And when towards the end of his life he needed a private and intimate service rendered it was to him he appealed inevitably. From their earliest acquaintance he sought him perpetually. "I am rather a pertinacious man (as we all of us who get through work must be) so I return to the charge. Can you come to us next Friday?" He was one of the early contributors to *Merry England* after an unpromising opening. "I will do something for it *if you like* but please understand I do not *want* to, having a superabundance of occupation"—and was soon signing a letter "Yours sempiternally, St. George for *Merry England.*" He began another letter "My dear Boy," and winds up "with mingled loves," adding: "If you *do* love me don't call me 'Professor!' Having left Louvain I now 'profess' nothing but I always remain a 'Saint.'" He watched the *Weekly Register* and complained in 1882 that it "was becoming a mere mouthpiece of the Cardinal." But in 1896 he commented on Manning's *Life*: "After all that can be said against it and its obvious gross faults, do you know I never knew how great a man Manning was till I had read it. It has raised him greatly in my eyes & Cardinal Wiseman also." He caught the *Register* tripping: "You think I do not read my Weekly R.! In today's number, about Central Africa, these words: 'So they got off with nothing worse than a fright. Lions & tigers,' adds Father Roelens, 'simply swarm here.' But unfortunately for Father Roelens—as regards accuracy—there are no tigers anywhere in Africa; the tiger is exclusively an Asiatic animal ranging from

China to islands of the Indian Archipelago." As a Fellow of the Zoological Society, with the privilege of giving passes for admission to the Zoo on Sundays, he showered them on the Meynell children and many still lie among his letters, in excess of what they could use. He had in Meynell a family man to deal with: "Wilfrido mio. After visiting your children you must come to your elder brother." And (in 1893): "Do not have your boy's tonsils cut out whatever happens. There seem to be grounds for believing that they eat up pernicious germs, bacteria, etc. which find their way into the mouth." His son was a doctor and he implored Meynell to use him when he ailed from overwork. He wrote in 1893 from Chilworth in Surrey: "I expect I have sold this place. I have got sick of it & of all the country round. There is no place I should not get sick of I am sure, & so we have made up our minds to live for a time *nowhere* that we may be the better able to enjoy *everywhere*. Everywhere has beauty, everywhere has charm except what you have just worn out, & with the nerves of your new-risen body that worn-out locality *must* be damnable. We hope like good snakes to shake off our old skins—& they shed even the skin of their eyes—by Xmas. Yours truly in metamorphosis . . ." And when he came to live round the corner from Palace Court: "No tongue can depict the hopeless muddle & confusion I am in here—where I have more than 2000 books, with more than three years dust on them, shot down in a room that may hold about 1200." They now shared a parish church and walked home together from the ten o'clock Mass at St. Mary's.

It was characteristically not with Wilfrid but with Alice Meynell that Mivart discussed problems of belief. She was alive to the formidable claims of science, protesting that "he who thinks that the religious difficulties suggested by astronomy, or geology, or physiology, or those which arise from the acute sensitiveness of the modern mind before the mysteries of evil and of eternal loss, are to be disposed of by a sneer at 'so-called science' or a smile at 'so-called philosophy,' has realized little indeed of the conditions of the physical or of the mental world in which he lives." She had keen understanding of those who "by

71

taking the sorrow and pain of life intimately to heart have unhappily begun to doubt the omnipotence of good." To such considerations on her part Mivart applied himself.

71 Seymour Street, Hyde Park, W.

My dear Mrs. Meynell,

The few words you said to me during our short walk on Saturday have dwelt in my memory ever since. I feel I must send you something on the matter we spoke of, though I cannot hope to present *you* with considerations which you have not long before either thought out for yourself or met with much better put than I can put them. Still a sympathetic word from a friend is sometimes more useful than a learned treatise.

Is it not an exaggeration to think that there is more ill than good in life? This it seems to me would be the case even if there were no compensation in another life or no complex system of interdependent actions beyond our ken producing even in this present world compensations & benefits no one dreams of.

To me as a student of nature, the material universe is a vast whole full to overflowing of a life which here & there reveals itself unmistakeably & shows plainly not only that all in it is order but that there is much of purpose in it. And when from the world without I turn to the world within I find myself the theatre & organ of an order & of purposes which are not mine to, & which I cannot, control. Turn as I may I cannot escape, not the blind impulsion but the clear perception that it is a *duty* to honour what is good & I cannot shut my eyes to the teaching of my conscience (that is my intellectual perception of what is right) that all "purposes" must be subordinate to *duty* & that therefore if there is a purpose in nature at all (& I know there are many) then that goodness—a goodness *essentially* similar to what I mean by goodness however different in degree & mode—must be highest & supreme over all the other purposes which I can conceive as underlying the phenomena of nature.

Reason tells me of a first cause even of the world even if it has been eternal, & reason also tells me that in the essence of that Cause there must be goodness. So I learn *a priori* & *a*

72

posteriori; & what have we on the other side? Nothing but a number (I confess a distressing number) of painful phenomena which we are bound to confess are the occasion of much good & of the *highest good* & which we have no reason whatever for saying may not be the necessary condition of the similitudes of goods of the highest kinds which as yet we cannot conceive of.

I will not weary you with more but I hope you may be able to agree with much of what I have said & if so what comfort results from it. What little unhappiness need arise from other religious difficulties is no complication if we may be sure of a good God. For there in history we have the wonderful unfolding of his nature through the Old Testament prophets culminating in Christ & his consoling preaching of the Fatherhood of God. In that have we not *everything*?

Very truly yours,
St. George Mivart

71 Seymour Street, Hyde Park, W.
5 Feb. 1885.

My dear Mrs. Meynell,

I was very pleased to receive your to me *very satisfactory* letter. The gist of my former letter (which I was too hurried I am afraid to make clear) was that as in our existing infinitesimally small knowledge of Nature we have come to apprehend multitudes of interactions & purposes for ages unsuspected, there is no reason against supposing that pain, suffering & our ethical perceptions may be interrelated & subservient to a great unknown end which if known would *abundantly* satisfy us. As to the difficulty you have spoken of—Revelation & Hell. I am *quite sure* that I can put your mind at rest & give you comfort though this cannot be done in this letter. I say I am quite sure because I have done the same for others. We must have a talk on this subject one day & meantime I trust you will take some little comfort from my *assurance* that you need feel no discomfort at all. Let Hell & damnation be entirely banished from your thoughts till we have our talk. Most certainly taken the way they are *commonly understood* they do not & cannot exist.

I am yours most truly,
St. G. Mivart

73

As an editor, Meynell had to comment on Mivart's opinions as they became extended in the articles he published in the *Fortnightly* and the *Nineteenth Century*. "My whole object," Mivart wrote to him, "is to keep liberal and intellectual men inside the Church." And again: "One thing you have most sagaciously divined—my satisfaction at the possible effect the thing may have, in strengthening my power for conciliation amongst Catholics. It may I trust also help me to get a hearing when I say that the Catholic cause is really the cause of Intellect versus Obscurantism." And: "I thank you very much indeed for your very kind article about me. It is of course far too eulogistic in my eyes but I suppose warm friendship is like love more or less blind to defects." But he had begun to be at strife with authority and suspicious of his own victimization a few months before his death. "My dear Wilfrid, Is it because the English & Irish Catholics so much desire my death that I did not receive from *you* a 'many happy returns' on the 30th? Evil desires towards me were so far successful that on my birthday I became unwell & am now laid up with a bilious attack which I think will very soon be a thing of the past. I should much like a chat with you alone."

Mivart's prolonged correspondence with Cardinal Vaughan on articles of faith, conducted with respect and patience on both sides, which Mivart sent to fill many columns of *The Times*, left him in an anomalous position, as to doctrine, on his death. It was a position which the Meynells, when his burial in consecrated ground was at stake, did everything in their power to explain and alleviate.

The last of Meynell's greatest friendships which are glanced at here was also the longest, because it was with one who was somewhat nearer his own age. Wilfrid Scawen Blunt was born twelve years before Meynell in 1840. He was educated at Stonyhurst and Oscott, his mother being a Catholic convert under Manning's influence. At eighteen he entered on a brief career in diplomacy, and that and a lung-illness in 1866 introduced him to his extensive travels. He brought his first Arab mares to England in 1878, and bred them henceforth on his Sussex estates. His nearly life-long struggle was in support of Irish, Indian and Egyptian Nationalism; his pamphlets, diaries and books show his rebel zeal, his poems his romanticism.

The first step in a friendship of forty-odd years was taken by Meynell in 1882.

The Weekly Register, 83 Fleet Street, London, E.C.
19 Aug. '82.

Dear Sir,

I venture to send you the last four copies of the *Register,* & if you have time to look into them you will see that we have followed your leadership in the Egyptian question; & we have done so without giving offence to one of our thousands of readers—which shows how little people really want the war.

As one who has read, always with deep interest, & sometimes with a much warmer sentiment, your works,—polemical, poetical, & political, I beg to thank you for the great pleasure & instruction they have afforded me.

My brother-in-law, Colonel Butler, who is out in Egypt on Sir Garnet Wolseley's staff has, you may be surprised to hear, read all that you have written on the Egyptian question, & with entire agreement.

I remain, dear Sir, Yours very faithfully,
Wilfrid Meynell

In 1885, when Blunt was Conservative candidate for North Camberwell, Indian reform being his "platform," Meynell organized a Catholic meeting in his support—a rare excursion for a non-party man. Blunt was not elected. Meynell's sympathy with Blunt's causes made him constantly his political fellow traveller.

Castello di Pavone, Canavese, Italy.
10 June 1900.

Dear Blunt,

Here, away from wars & rumours of wars, I feel able for the first time to thank you for the last book—by this time in one sense an old story. In the nature of the case, however, such a book does not really belong to the date at which it is written, but to the future. This national deafness! When it has gone, which may be long hence, your book will remain as one of very few evidences of a feeling among our contemporaries which finds no expression in the journalism of the day, & which is not allowed an echo in the shape of an appreciation of your book, even in papers that are supposed to be conducted by men of ideas, & not dependent on popular support.

We have been in Italy a month &, having moved about, are lacking all news, even as to the War. This is an old mediaeval Castle, belonging to some Italian relations of ours, & dominating a little town of peasant proprietors whose life, nevertheless, is a very hard one, especially when as now the thunderstorms daily destroy their crops & vines & threaten their Indian corn & hemp. The church bells ring out an appeal to Heaven during the storms, alas in vain.

Believe me, most truly yours,
Wilfrid Meynell

He was quick on the mark with any London news for his friend. In April, 1907, he telegraphed to Blunt in the country the news of Cromer's resignation as Resident in Egypt six months after the Denshawai affair, when Egyptian villagers, after a quarrel with seven officers of the Army of Occupation about the shooting of the villagers' tame pigeons, were savagely punished. Blunt's telegraphic reply was "Who-whoop." Meynell was a favourite with Blunt who sought him constantly for his company's sake; he also performed his usual function of expert adviser on printing and publishing.

In Wilfrid Blunt's *My Diaries*, published in 1918 and 1919, the words "Meynell tells me" occur again and again as prelude to some piece of information. Any rumour from the "inside" in the world of politics or of religion, one Wilfrid was, it must be owned, as ready to give as the other Wilfrid to receive. Or even, in 1901: "To see Meynell who was as usual full of gossip. It appears that the King's debts have been paid off privately," etc. But whether in the telling or in the writing down by Blunt, reports sometimes went astray from accuracy; and in Meynell's annotated copy of the *Diaries* he has written "Not so" in the margin beside some of these entries. One of the things "Meynell tells me," when Meynell saw it on first receiving his copy of the *Diaries*, so dismayed him that an emergency appeal was made to the publisher, Martin Secker, for correction, who gave Meynell the assurance that "it should not take more than 24 hours to print a small slip to qualify or to rectify the expression of any statements attributed to you, and directly I hear from Mr. Blunt I will see to it." Blunt had written in his diary in 1892:

Meynell told me also of a new movement within the body of the English Catholic clergy, of the most revolutionary kind, especially among the Capuchins, and that the Cardinal in some measure sympathized with it. A movement of the widest sort, rationalistic and mystic, which embraced all forms of religion and repudiated the finality of any doctrine of the Church, a kind of positivism and creed of humanity, in which Plato, and Buddha, and Mohammed were alike canonized as saints, and Christ himself hardly more than these. He assured me that such doctrines were widely held by the younger priests, and that some of their most zealous and able exponents were to be found among our monks at Crawley. It was no heresy, he said, and the General of the Capuchins who had come from Rome to put it down had gone back converted. This sounds to me altogether incredible, but he promised to send me the writings of the new creed in print.—Meynell's talk has done me good. It opens to me a view of a religious position, not absolutely illogical, in which I may still be loyal to all my ideas without quarrelling with the Catholic Church. I mean to talk the matter over with Father Cuthbert, the young Capuchin at our monastery, whom Meynell speaks of as the leading light of the new doctrine.

On a fly-leaf of the *Diaries* Meynell has made a pencilled note:

I read with understanding and sympathy Frederic Harrison's letter to *The Times* written after he had read his friend Sir Algernon West's allusions to him in his published Memoirs. Nobody can quote correctly (often after a lapse of days or weeks) the opinions expressed in general conversation. Even

77

where correctly reproduced, they acquire a false stress by their isolation from their context and from the talk of others leading up to them. Sometimes what one has said of *A* is attributed to *B,* as for instance in the talk about the religious sentiments of the Capuchins. Of this confusion I was obliged to ask my dear friend to insert my disclaimer, which he readily did. Other inaccuracies did not so much matter, & they remain.

W. M.

The printed slip inserted in the volume stated: "Mr. Meynell tells me that I unintentionally misrepresent the views held by Father Cuthbert and his friends. 'Not one,' he says in particular, 'of that fervent group of young Franciscans but fixed all his hope and all his faith on the doctrine, fundamental and final, of the divinity of Christ.' "

But of these same *Diaries* Meynell wrote to Blunt in 1919:

> The Book has kept me in its thrall. I cannot in a few words say all I think & feel about it, especially what I feel. You have been in *deed* what England now is in word—the friend of small peoples, & you must take at least the comfort of finding lip-service given to the ideals that are yours. That they are Christian ideals, however imperfectly recognized as such, I am sure; & I therefore mourn the more that you who should be our protagonist speak as it were from the outside. We did, & do, need you so badly.

Blunt and Meynell had a few points of literary difference. Meynell was a Stevensonian, Blunt did not like him well enough even to spell his name right. "I took away with me, without intending to, that volume of Stephenson's you gave me to read at night, the night I slept under your roof, and I hereby return it," he wrote in 1903. "With the exception of *Treasure Island* I am not a particular devotee of Stephenson's stories & but for your recommendation I doubt if I shd. have got through *Prince Otto*. As it is I read it but without enthusiasm." Blunt's hospitality at interesting dinners in Chapel Street and week-ends at Crabbet and then at the beautiful Jacobean "Newbuildings" near Horsham afforded Meynell his life's chief social pleasure. The yearly sales, until the First World War, of Arab horses at the Crabbet stud were the outing-event of the year for the Meynell family, for they included an enormous luncheon-party in a marquee. "Over 400 people," Blunt wrote, "have accepted the invitations, including 2 Maharajahs, a Sultan, a Royal Highness, & 20 Colonial bigwigs, a regular bag-full. I send also a card for Francis Thompson if he is get-at-able."

That he was not. About this invitation he wrote, characteristically, to Palace Court: "Had it been last Saturday I would have gone," adding: "I shall soon be level with arrears of work which have so worried me, together with the legacy of ill-health from the most disastrous winter (as regards its physical effects) I have known since I left the streets." Before this, in 1898, Blunt had written to Meynell: "I will remind you that you have often promised me that I shd. make Thompson's acquaintance"—and his *Diaries* record the keeping of the promise in that same year.

12th Oct. A visit from Mrs. Meynell and her husband and Francis Thompson at Newbuildings. I had invited them to come for the night, but Meynell had explained that this was impossible, "the poet having an inconvenient habit of setting his bed on fire." They came down, however, for the day. I met them at the station, a very lovely day, and as we drove through the woods Meynell pointed out to me that "the poet of nature" was wholly absorbed in the *Globe* newspaper he had brought down with him in the train. Thompson, though born in Lancashire and speaking English with a broad provincial accent, is a true Cockney. He is a little weak-eyed, red-nosed young man of the degenerate London type, with a complete absence of virility and a look of raptured dependence on Mrs. Meynell which is most touching. He is very shy, but was able to talk a little when the general conversation was not too loud, and he seems good-hearted and quite unpretending. He has written no poetry, Meynell tells me, now for some years, being cured of his morphia. But Meynell thinks the fountain may some day break forth again. Meanwhile, he gets a living by literary criticism in the *Academy* and other journals. When we all went out after luncheon to the

79

woods, I found him quite ignorant of the names of the commonest trees, even the elm, which he must have seen every day in London. I pointed one out to him, and he said, "I think, a maple." On the whole, however, I liked him, for he was quite simple and straightforward. Only, it was difficult to think of him as capable of any kind of strength in rhyme or prose. Meynell has greatly improved conversationally with years, and has become a most agreeable man. Thanks to him, the visit was a pleasant one and they all went home in spirits.

The acquaintance thus made went no further until nine years later, when Blunt and Thompson had a singularly close connection.

In 1911, when Meynell was able to launch out into a small country house in eighty acres of land not far from Storrington, Blunt welcomed him as the host warmly receiving a guest into Sussex. "I am delighted to hear of your having bought near so delightful a place as Parham. Also, the distance from here, 10 miles, will make it a pleasant outing for us"—though he also regretted that "now you have your own country seat I suppose I shall see no more of you here." Living much in Egypt he brought something of his outdoor, tent-pitching life into England, suppressing cultivation near his house (a trait infectious to Meynell) and driving his four-in-hand, dressed in a white Bagdad robe becoming to his great good looks. "I hope to get together a team of Arabs," he wrote, "which will put Greatham into easier reach" —and he flattered Meynell's new proprietorship: "I drove over to Greatham last Sunday with Cockerell but found you flown. We went back by Rackham and Storrington and noticed many rabbits & partridges while crossing your manor."

Blunt's wife, Lady Anne, was the daughter of Byron's daughter Ada and her husband the Earl of Lovelace. With Blunt's literary and political and many-nationed friends Meynell was brought into conjunction. "A glorious day here," he wrote home, "& very pleasant talk with A. E. Housman & our host & Desmond McCarthy who is writing a play with Belloc. I was made to read *Modern Love* aloud last night—rather an ordeal before

80

strangers who could have done it so much better." Blunt's comment on the occasion in his diary was: "We had a poetical evening, Meynell reading us 'Modern Love,' with a running commentary, an excellent entertainment, as good as the best of lectures." In October, 1912, Blunt wrote to Meynell: "Since seeing you I have been ten days in Worth Forest entertaining my guests, Winston among others. He was very amusing & interesting, though gone imperialistically altogether to the dogs. I am in despair about Oriental things & feel that that Chapter of my life is at an end. If there is anything more to hope it will not be in my time or in any way that I can help to realize."

In the years just before the First World War Blunt was in his seventies and his health was breaking up, and he often called himself a lonely man with much need of his friend.

Newbuildings Place, Southwater, Sussex.

June 27, 1913.

Dear Meynell,

It dismays me to hear of your being ill in bed in London all this time that I was thinking of you at Greatham enjoying the June weather & the view of the Downs. I cannot afford to have you invalided, for this has been a grievous year for me & I counted on you for consolation & encouragement—not for new anxieties. Illness, however, & even pain, have their own kind of happiness (I experienced that seven years ago) and I am glad to know that you have yours now, & convalescence when it comes is one of the sweetest & most delicate pleasures of life, as you will find. I have been following your public fortunes with close interest, both in the matter of the laureateship,[1] which you may remember was originally my idea, or if not originally, suggested by me some months before there was any talk of it in print; & in that of the Thompson publication.[2] . . . I read the prose volume first, & it raised my opinion immensely of Thompson as a man of sound critical taste. There are original truths in the estimates he makes of other poets which delight

---

[1] There was a suggestion that the laureateship, which had been left vacant since Tennyson's death, should be filled by Alice Meynell.

[2] *The Works of Francis Thompson*, in three volumes, one of them prose.

me, though I do not agree with them always. Verse however was clearly his birthright, and I am quite ready to say that, Swinburne excepted and perhaps Rossetti, he is our greatest lyric poet since Shelley & Keats. He has more substance in him than any of them—I mean intellectual substance. I remember expressing to you long ago that he was an original theologian. We may yet see the first steps taken towards his canonisation! . . .

Yours ever,
Wilfrid Scawen Blunt

In May, 1914, he wrote: "Belloc says we are to be invaded next week, but fortunately not by way of the Sussex Downs." With the onset of the war Meynell reaffirmed their bond, writing in October, 1914: "I cannot tell you how much pleasure & interest —I will say joy & riches—you have added to my life by *your* life & writings. Words will not express my gratitude;—but you must know that my affection for you does in some way embody it." Blunt fed his friends from his farms and forests. "Shall I send you a peacock for your Xmas dinner? If properly cooked they are good." In 1916 the two friends mourned over Casement's fate. Blunt wrote:

> I have just heard from Miss Bannister [Roger Casement's cousin] that she has been able to convey to Casement in prison [Pentonville] the subject of my letter to you, & that it has pleased him. Though I cannot have anything to do with a plea ad misericordiam on the ground of insanity which wd. be too stupid I have decided to write to Asquith as the person most responsible expressing my great admiration of Casement & my opinion of the shame he will personally incur in history if Casement is executed or granted less than a free pardon. I gather that Casement himself is prepared for a full martyrdom, and it would be doing him a cruel wrong for his friends by any unworthy display of weakness to rob him of his crown.

In December, 1917, he wrote: "Things I think look more hopeful now for a peace on reasonable terms such as the Pope proposes. I should like to see the Peace Congress of 1918 held at the Vatican.

I feel as if I could almost write a short article to that effect for your *Dublin* Xmas number." And in September, 1918:

> Every day for the last fortnight I have looked at the sky & thought of Greatham as a possible venture & every day the clouds have risen & the rain has fallen & now the days have grown short & the world too cold. So I shall miss visiting you any more this year—perhaps for ever. The truth is I cannot keep warm out of doors except for a very short time & then go to bed, for my blood refuses to circulate even at the news of the British marching into Nazareth or Lloyd George having compounded matters with the railway strikers or fixed a day for the General Election. I wrap myself the more tightly in the recollection that I was once an early Victorian youth in peg top trousers with ladies who played croquet in crinolines. But the glory of all things fades. I shall try to fire a gun on the 1st of October & if I succeed I will send you a pheasant.

In May, 1921, he wrote: "All seems to be going as badly in the world as people with ideas like yours & mine had thought beyond the possibility of evil." He died in the following year. Extreme Unction was administered to him on his deathbed, but his will had provided for his burial "wrapped in my old Eastern travelling carpet and without coffin or casket of any kind in a spot in Newbuildings wood known to my executors without religious ceremony or the intervention of strangers but by men employed on my Newbuildings Estate."

Meynell adopted for his own use Sir Henry Taylor's "I prefer any woman to any man"—and not entirely for the *mot* quality of it, but as a romantic-minded man who had friendships with women of conspicuous beauty and charm. To those whose very attractions had perhaps been the cause of hitherto uninspiring contacts he appeared as the opener of a new world of chivalry, with disinterested exchange of ideas, confidences, and poetry-reading, in a bond which brought him lifelong devotion.

A thing he inspired in his friends was reliance, the confidence that what was needed would be given. Of the love which means service he had plenty to give, and he was fast-acting in any practical need. He was a man around whom natural affections prevailed, given and received. His brother Samuel was a businessman in Newcastle, from whom he was separated by distance, and in work and outlook and religion. But letters tell their own tale and one of them from Samuel ends: "Do not fail to believe, dear Wilfrid, how much such a life as yours consoles and sustains your very affectionate brother S. T. M. Your verses move my heart."

VII

FRANCIS THOMPSON must have been known to fewer people than anyone has ever been who achieved so much fame. In London a series of landladies in the Harrow Road region knew him; a few fellow lodgers; the editors of the *Academy* and the *Athenaeum*, for which he wrote, and a few of the Meynells' friends, though less than they intended. "Dear Wilfrid," he wrote, "I could not come in to tea with Blunt & Yeats, for I had to go down to the *Academy*, & was back much too late. Had I known on Thursday I would have altered my arrangements so as to accept your invitation. I am very sorry to have missed this chance of meeting Yeats, as I have long desired to do. You know I heartily admire his work." The plausible explanation would impress only someone who was not familiar with the repetition of it in many forms on many occasions. It certainly impressed Thompson himself, for he always believed in the insuperable obstacles which he described. Acquaintance between him and George Meredith began and ended with a night's visit to Boxhill in 1896. Meredith had written from there to Alice Meynell: "You and the poet will have Heaven's welcome to the elect." But Meredith and Thompson can have viewed each other only with respectful and alien interest. Normal approaches made to Thompson as a man of importance were wide of the mark. Elliott and Fry wished to photograph him "in his study." An American woman-poet on a visit to London suggested that he should sometimes go to her "for a quiet talk *à deux*." A journalist wished to interview him as a "Celebrity at Home." Such were the requests arriving at the ugly lodging-house room where he lay in bed half the day.

But he was a man of the warmest outpouring of affection.

It was my practice from the time I left college to pray for the lady whom I was destined to love—the unknown She. It is curious that even then I did not dream of praying for her whom I was destined to marry; & yet not curious; for already I had previsioned that with me it would be to love, not to be loved —thus he wrote in a notebook in reference to one of his poems.

But a lover has acute awareness—of another and of himself; and Thompson was that rare thing, a man of such complete unselfconsciousness, in the ordinary sense of the word, that in the company of others both he and they remained in a sense alone. The protective guard which acknowledges the presence of other people was in his case lacking, leaving him—as a child is—open to free observation; he was never watching. Any onlooker knew more of his repetitive movements than he himself knew—a brushing upward movement at his scanty moustache, right and left; his shoulders hitching up his coat; the striking and re-striking of matches in the attempt to light his pipe, and his hand feeling in his coat pocket for something—his eyes showed he had forgotten what. He was not fully present. So much did he give the impression of someone not pinned down to any place or moment that for one who remembers him only thus it is even difficult, when reading a bit of plain-stated literary criticism written by him, or his carefully composed letters, to link them with the man who in company was mostly silent or repetitive or irrelevant, and never effectual. (It seems more easy to leave his poetry unexplained than his reasoned prose.)

In 1890, writing to the family friend of his Manchester days, he says: "Good Uncle Edward [Healy Thompson] styled 'Dream-tryst' as erotic. I charitably suppose him to have merely meant that it was a love-poem. As a matter of fact 'Dream-tryst' is not a love-poem (though I admit it reads like one). It could not be a love-poem, for I never in my life was in love." But it was not a subject of which he would have professed ignorance. He started on the basis that "all human love is to me a symbol of divine love. The one is illustrated by the other." He was not afraid to analyse the nature of man's love in contrast with that of a woman, whose capacity, he insisted, was insufficient to respond to a pure and lofty lover. "Though she cast her whole self down

that eager gulf, it would disappear as a water-drop in the ocean."
He could probe the married history of Shelley, the married
happiness of Browning when he "stooped and picked up a fair-
coined soul that lay rusting in a pool of tears." But love as applied
to himself? Writing to Alice Meynell concerning doctrines of
Coventry Patmore's on marriage, from which he withheld agreement, he adds the speculation as to himself: "Provided I were
united with a woman's spirit I would be content to wait for her
body till I could be united with it on the same terms—*i.e.* as a
spirit, when it was assumed to the dignity of its soul. I recognise
that on earth it may not be so for the many."

If as a result he could have been saved from all wounds of love
it would have been just; and in fact what he suffered must have
been not in the whole-world of the pain of unrequited love but
in the half-world only of his limited conception of any possible
bond. His love of Alice Meynell, who was twelve years older
than himself, was, as has been said, mostly a distant worship even
within a daily intimacy. The distance was composed of his own
nature and hers, he a man knowing he was "not to be loved," she
a woman bound to be loved, but whose own love was consecrated to husband and family. He addressed her:

> My restless wings that beat the whole world through
> Flag on the confines of the sun and you,
> And find the human pale remoter of the two.

His brooding on her was in terms of his poetry, and there he
could bestow a kind of eternal life on them both.

> I sprinkled a few drops of verse,
> And said to Ruin, "Quit thy hearse:"
>   To my Loved, "Pale not, come with me;
> I will escort thee down the years,
>   With me thou walk'st immortally."

He dealt out his high compliments to her poetry, and to the
sanctity he saw in her, calling these two the Tables of her double
Law, and in "To a Poet Breaking Silence" he implores her not

to fall on poetic silence but to unite the songs of "both her countries."

> Too wearily had we and song
> Been left to look and left to long,
> Yea, song and we to long and look,
> Since thine acquainted feet forsook
> The mountain where the Muses hymn
> For Sinai and the Seraphim.
> Now in both the mountains' shine
> Dress thy countenance, twice divine!
> From Moses and the Muses draw
> The Tables of thy double Law!
> His rod-born fount and Castaly
> Let the one rock bring forth for thee,
> Renewing so from either spring
> The songs which both thy countries sing:
> Or we shall fear lest, heavened thus long,
> Thou should'st forget thy native song,
> And mar thy mortal melodies
> With broken stammer of the skies.
>
> Ah! let the sweet birds of the Lord
> With earth's waters make accord;
> Teach how the crucifix may be
> Carven from the laurel-tree,
> Fruit of the Hesperides
> Burnish take on Eden-trees,
> The Muses' sacred grove be wet
> With the red dew of Olivet,
> And Sappho lay her burning brows
> In white Cecilia's lap of snows! . . .

Only occasionally the heart-burning of a more pressing and pained emotion was expressed.

British Museum.
Saturday Evening.

Dear Mrs. Meynell,

I am unhappy when I am out of your sight; and would pass every hour, if I could, in your exquisite presence, only to feel ye effluence of your spirit in contact with mine. But *you*, of course, can have no such feeling in reference to me; and would often gladly be without my presence when my love for you prompts it, and your good nature prompts you patiently to bear it. Now my sense of this inspires me with a continual timidity about inflicting my society on you in any way, unless you in some way signify a desire for it. Hence such misunderstandings as that of today.

Let this be sufficient, & let it not come between us. I know how it must tax you to endure me; for you are a friend, a mother; while I, over & above these, am a lover—spiritual as light, and unearthly as ye love of one's angelic dreams, if you will—but yet a lover; and even a seraph enamoured must be a trying guardian-angel to have to do with.

Ahi! soavissima Madonna Alice, avete pieta di me!

> Ever yours, most beloved lady,
>   Francis Thompson

One letter (delivered by his own hand as many of his letters to the Meynells were) begins peaceably. During a few days' absence, in one of her rare letters to him, she had called him "friend and child."

> 1 Fernhead Road,
>   Paddington, W.

Dear Mrs. Meynell,

Your sudden arrival on Tuesday prevented me from answering your letter—the letter from Anglesey—but I resolved nevertheless, as soon as the *Register* permitted, to tell you how delighted I was to receive that letter. Indeed, after you left, I felt as if it were night, with a great hole in the heavens where the moon ought to be. The concluding words of your letter, "friend & child," reminded me of some lines written at the time I was composing *Amphicypellon*. They were written hastily, to relieve an outburst of emotion; and, not thinking there was any poetry in them worthy of you, I never showed them you. But when I read those concluding words of your letter, I remembered the lines; and resolved to transcribe them, that you might see you could not have addressed me more according to my wish.

The transcribed lines were these; they had been written after the Meynells' visit to Thompson at Storrington in 1889.

In her Paths[1]

And she has trod before me in these ways!
I think that she has left here heavenlier days;
And I do guess her passage, as the skies
    Of holy Paradise
    Turn deeply holier,
And, looking up with sudden new delight,
One knows a seraph-wing has passed in flight.

The air is purer for her breathing, sure!
    And all the fields do wear
    The beauty fallen from her;
The winds do brush me with her robe's allure.
'Tis she has taught the heavens to look sweet
    And they do but repeat
The heaven, heaven, heaven of her face!
The clouds have studied going from her grace!
The pools whose marges had forgot the tread
Of Naiad, disenchanted, fled,
    A second time must mourn,
    Bereaven and forlorn.

Ah, foolish pools and meads! You did not see
Essence of old, essential pure as she.
For this was even that Lady, and none other,
The man in me calls "Love," the child calls "Mother."

The letter continues:

Madam has been worse than I anticipated, and told me something which has left me very unhappy. I fear, indeed, I shall hardly sleep.

                        Ever your own,
                           Francis

I hope you are going to have no headaches, but to be just happy for a while, now the *Register* is done. And that to-

[1] Printed in *Merry England* in 1893, and posthumously published in the *Collected Works*.

morrow, for once in a way, and Saturday, you will do just what you like and take pleasure in doing: if, indeed, it is possible to you for one day to drop that inveterate habit of thinking so much of other people, that you put yourself away in a corner and forget that you have left yourself there. And since I think you must have had far too much of my company forced upon you during the last fortnight, if I leave you now as much as may be without me you must ascribe it solely to my anxiety for anything which might fatigue you; not to neglect, of which I am incapable, or weariness, which no man —I least—could feel in your companionship.

Friday noon. I intended this to go to you last night, but it was too late: so I leave it behind me this afternoon. I had first of all written a note of very different character, in which I told you what Madam had said,[1] and asked you, if you could, to reassure me. But I decided not to send it, on a re-reading. Firstly, I began to doubt whether it might not be a breach of Madam's confidence, in a certain way. Secondly, because, being written in the full rush of feeling after what I had heard, it was so vehemently emotional that I feared you might at once despise & be troubled by it. Yet I confess after all I have some doubt whether it had not better have gone. I have suffered so from reticence all my life: and the opening out of hearts & minds, where there is confidence, puts an end to so much secret trouble that would grow monstrous if it were brooded over.

I will be back for dinner this evening.

Such rare turmoils might have survived humouring arguments on her part; they could not survive her detachment and reserve, and fell into oblivion. And Thompson's poetry concerning her is full of the power and glory of praise without repining. Their common absorbed interest in literature and in origins and metres was a normal meeting ground. "My dear Francis,—The Bible has 'unquenchable,' and I don't think it could have 'quenchless.' Lowell has 'exhaustless' somewhere. I think one can strictly hold 'less' to equal 'minus' or 'without,' and with these the verb is

---

[1] Some disquiet not now to be traced.

impossible. I remember refusing to be taught a setting of some work of Praed's that had 'tameless' for 'untamable,' so you see it is an old objection with me. I must confess that 'dauntless' has taken a very firm place in the language." That such subjects never lost interest between them is shown by one of the last letters of Thompson's life. He had detected her hand in a paragraph in the *Daily Chronicle*. "Dear Mrs. Meynell,—You might have added to the *willow* par. the Latin *salex* & the English *sallow*. The English, I should guess, may be from one of the Romance Tongues; if so all these modern forms are, mediately or immediately, from the Latin. But it is interesting to find the Latin & the Irish really identical (if you neglect the inflectional endings in the former) salic & salagh," etc. Her attitude to Thompson had always been peculiarly impersonal. She met him most in literature.

Before returning to London life, and while he was still at Pantasaph, the last of his lodgings was at Creccas Cottage with the Briens, those of whom he had written "people that I know & like, & who will not want to get rid of me on account of my erratic ways." The manner of his first acquaintance with the Briens can be gathered from a letter to Meynell:

If the reviews I send are not very brilliant, you must excuse me if you can; for I myself am not very brilliant just now. Fact is, the dearest child has made friends with me in the park; & we have fallen in love with each other with an instantaneous rapidity not unusual on my side, but a good deal more unusual on the child's. I rather fancy she thinks me one of the most admirable of mortals; & I firmly believe her to be one of the most daintily supernatural of fairies. And now I am in a fever lest (after the usual manner of fairies) her kinsfolk should steal her from me. Result—I haven't slept for two nights, & I fear I shall not recover myself until I am resolved whether my glimpses of her are to be interdicted or not. Of course in some ways she is sure to vanish; elves always do, & my elves in particular. This individual little elf is a Catholic, by the way; which partly accounts for the celerity of our mutual confidence. And her kinsfolk see the *Register* every week; which ought to throw for you a new & agreeable light upon Elfland.

Or was it he who was the elf? A tentative romance, as she grew into girlhood, with the shy young Maggie Brien, whose reticence was both natural and trained, could prompt in Thompson at any rate his symbolic thesis of womanhood as the "narrow vessel" unable to contain love in man's degree. But the agitation of this mutual attraction did not surpass its beginnings. There was something of the fearful, shy, deceiving game of hiding and finding ("I hope your father doesn't want the proof of my portrait back," Thompson was writing to Monica Meynell, "because a girl at my lodgings has gone off with it, I'm sure I don't know why, for she does not like me, & keeps out of my way as much as possible"); and then it died—no doubt of elfin-ness. But Maggie Brien treasured this portrait of him in her cottage-room long after he had gone, and her emotion, unlikely in its object as first love may be, must have loomed large in her short life—she died in the October following Thompson's death, a young woman, and was laid in a poor grave namelessly in the Pantasaph churchyard.

So Thompson was evidently not completely stamped with his immunity from romance. If he had been, his friendship with another girl, Katharine Douglas King, need never have made him seem to trespass into that strange land. But it appears that even he was subject to the conventions of the time by which friendship between the marriageable of opposite sexes had to be a matter for immediate definition. Katie King was the daughter of Mrs. Hamilton King, whose poems had some religious and political power, and who told the story of her long and fervent discipleship in her *Letters and Recollections of Mazzini*, edited by G. M. Trevelyan. Mrs. Hamilton King was a delicate woman confined mostly to her couch, noble-minded, red-haired and pre-Raphaelite-looking. Of her large family Katie was the one who inherited a writing talent. In 1894 Mrs. Hamilton King had written to Meynell: "I am very glad you think well of my daughter's stories; I naturally see their weak points, especially the tendency to exaggerate trifles, & to be always at the highest pitch of agony. Of course they are little tragedies but still there should

93

be gradations. She has some real knowledge of East-end life, for she spends one day & sometimes more every week at a little East-end Hospital for incurable & dying children, & enters into both their lives & deaths." Two years later Thompson was writing from Pantasaph:

Do you know that Miss K. Douglas King is—together with Winifred Lucas[1]—the only one of your female friends I ever desired particularly to meet? I have a vivid interest in her. She has the temperament of genius heaped up and running over. I read through all her *Merry England* stories some months ago; and was startled by their individual and impressive note. I admired them strongly—not, I think, for that which she would desire to be admired in them. I think she would claim admiration for their realism. I admire them for their idealism. In all the chief characters there is something which never was in any such character. And that something is Miss King. This, for which most would reprobate her, I admire. It is the light which never was on sea or land. Her weak point is a feminine tendency to pile up the agony, heaping one emotional touch upon another, until the accumulated effect is overstrung. Some French novelists gain pathos by accumulated touches. But then the touches are carefully minor and unimpressive singly; so that the pathos gains on you imperceptibly as a mist. Where the artist's tendency is to work by poignant detail there should be reserve and selection in quantity. . . . There is a very striking and attractive individuality disclosed through all these stories. If it is of any value to her, pray convey to her my sincere admiration of her true gift.

So when Thompson came to stay at Palace Court during the Pantasaph period—and he came sometimes for as much as two months at a time—he met Katie King. Writing to Coventry Patmore he allowed himself a boast:

I have come to London for a month. I hope I may see you before I leave here. Am already engaged to go to George

---

[1] Poet. She later became Mrs. Le Bailly.

Meredith's for a day, while a girl I have met here wants me to visit her; which is pretty fair for the very evening one reaches town.

Katie King was a well-loved visitor at Palace Court—a sensitive, vivacious, nearly pretty girl, with nodding flowers in her hat, and her skirt brushing the ground as she went her eager way to the children's hospital, and with an attractive manner of complete unaffectedness. After their meetings they corresponded on terms of friendship and Thompson addressed verses to her. He also became friendly with her mother. His feelings, involved from the beginning, made him susceptible to severe irritation and disappointment; back at Pantasaph he was again writing to Patmore:

Until this week the only persons besides yourself who had shown any recollection of my existence were two ladies, mother and daughter, whose acquaintance I made only during my recent London visit. They surprised and touched me very much by both writing very charming and delicate letters of regret at my sudden departure. That was a very absurd and annoying situation in which I was placed by W. M.'s curious methods of handling me. He never let me know that my visit was about to terminate until the actual morning I was to leave for Lymington. The result was that I found myself in the ridiculous position of having made a formal engagement by letter for the next week, only two days before my final departure from London. Luckily both women knew my position and if anyone suffered in their opinion it was not I.

But these were days when not only must a girl's fair name be protected but she must never, by the merest shade of over-friendliness, risk inflicting pain by giving grounds for "hope" where none was justified. The avoidance of this was a responsibility shared, or shouldered, by parents. And Mrs. Hamilton King, worrying on her sofa, wrote to Thompson assuring him that he must not be deceived into thinking that Katie would ever love

95

him. His reply, which no longer exists, must have disclaimed the idea of any woman loving him. Mrs. King wrote:

> Forest Hall, Hale End, Essex.
> Oct. 31st, 1896.

My dear Francis,

I cannot help writing to you at once. I thank you from my heart for your letter, which makes me honour you & value your friendship more than ever. It was a great pain to me to write, & to feel *your* pain, & yet I felt it was necessary. Certainly your letters & poems were open to misconstruction, though only of the most honourable kind; & I am thankful for the frank explanation.

As for Katie herself she has all along held your view simply & calmly. She expostulated at first when I told her I thought I must write in the sense I did, but she yielded to my opinion. I showed her my letter, & she made no demur to it; but she was entirely passive. What you say about her being likely to enter a convent has been often in my own mind, though it is very painful to me.

It is not in her nature to love you; but I see no reason why some other good woman should not;—yet perhaps you are most fitted to live & die solitary, & in the love only of the Highest Lover, whom you yourself in your supreme moments feel to have espoused you to Himself. The solitary life has many advantages.

As for Katie she has never changed to you at all; she has simply submitted to what I thought right. She is at present staying in the Convent. Still I think that at this moment it would be better not to re-commence a correspondence which I believe has been dropped for some weeks; for she has lately seemed wholly engrossed in her work. But I can see no reason why you should not meet again, now that this frank explanation has been made, & no one can misunderstand.

I have not seen her letters to you, not wishing at her age to invade her privacy; & I have not asked to see yours, but she has shown me *most* of them. It would seem best as you have destroyed her letters to do the same by yours. Letters are but fugitive.

As for myself I am afraid I have as little worldly wisdom as you have; I have not enough for my position; many things have forced me to be a recluse. Indeed I feel that both my daughter & I are honoured by your friendship; & I could not part from it without still more pain.

Affectionately yours,
H. E. Hamilton King

Four months later Katie herself wrote to Thompson now established in London:

Forest Hall, Hale End, Woodford Green.
Feb. 8, '97.

My dear Francis,

I have long been wanting to give you a photograph of myself, & now I hope you will accept this one. I heard you are at Palace Court again. I have been wanting to write to you for a long time, but I thought I would not write to you directly after my mother. I did not want to add (as I fear any words of mine would have done) to the pain & disappointment that letter must have brought you. I say disappointment because I think you must have been disappointed as well as grieved to find that after all I had apparently not understood & rejoiced in your friendship for me. But indeed I think I did understand it, & it certainly was a great joy & pride to me to know you were my friend.

And I should like you to know that I was very sorry indeed that owing to the intervention & as I think misrepresentations of others—even with the best & kindest intents—our friendship has received so severe, unwarrantable & unnecessary a check. My wish was against a letter going to you. I thought we—you & I—understood each other perfectly—& it turns out we did!

I am a great deal at the little children's Hospital. Mr. Meynell knows the way. I know you are very busy now, you are writing a great deal & your book is coming out, isn't it? but if you are able & care to come, you know how glad I shall be.

Ever yours sincerely,
Katharine Douglas King

Thompson preserved her frank affectionate letters written for some years after the "explanation" to his lodging-house addresses: 39 Goldney Road, Harrow Road; 16 Elgin Avenue. This one is written a month after the one above. He had now visited her at the hospital.

Forest Hall, Hale End, Woodford Green.
March 31.

My dear Francis,

I have been thinking often of you since Saturday, & wondering how you are. I am afraid you may have had an attack of influenza which is so much about, & with that you must take care, the greatest care, & I am afraid you do not take enough care of yourself. Your visit on Saturday tells me this again! I was very glad to see you again, Francis, & see for myself from your face & know from your ready hand-clasp that we are friends—not "again" but "still," & I hope always. I count you as an old friend now, but I know now I did not really know you until Saturday. When you were by the bed of your little "genius," Harry; & the baby boy, Percy, with the white shoes, was at your knee, that was to me a revelation! I think of you now with that baby boy's serious confiding face upturned to you. It was all so *natural*. For some people a child is a pretty ornamental addition. Your personality now seems incomplete without the child as the natural & exquisite finish to the whole man. Adieu dear friend.

Yours ever sincerely,
Katharine D. King

She was prolifically producing books during these years: *The Scripture-Reader of St. Marks*; *Father Hilarion*, etc. This is the last of her letters to Thompson:

Forest Hall.
April 11, 1900.

My dear Francis,

I have been wanting to write to you for so long; & now I find it a little difficult because one feels reluctant to speak of one's own great happiness to one whose life has been so sad

& lonely as yours, even though that one should be so firm & true a friend as you have ever been to me.

Perhaps you may have heard that I am engaged to be married to Mr. Godfrey Burr, vicar of Rushall near Walsall in Staffordshire; & our marriage is fixed for the early part of July. Although my new home will be far away we both hope that in time we may come to live nearer London, & I hope that my marriage will bring me not less but more in touch with my friends, amongst whom, Francis, I hope that I may ever count you as one of the first & nearest. Goodbye, dear Francis, & may God bless you.

Yours always affectionately,
Katharine D. King

His impression of Katie King was recorded thus by Thompson:

There is no need of courage in the feminine woman, and I love her for the fact. Yet my dear friend (now removed by marriage) was a brave woman, and I loved her for it against all my wont. Perhaps, because she took me by surprise; perhaps because—who knows why? She was not self-reliant with all her bravery, and I suppose the combination made her real femininity the more piquant. Perhaps it was rather her crystal truth than the courage which (I think) came from it, not caused it, that won me at sight. Truth—*integrity* (or oneness) *of nature* is what calls to me.

Her marriage had taken place in July, 1900; in the following April she was dead in childbirth.

The story of the extent to which women figured in Thompson's life has soon been completed. They barely touched the solitude of a man alone.

And, apart from Meynell, he had almost nothing of man's companionship, though two men came so close to him through his poetry that they enriched his life with however little personal contact. One was a man of dynamic personality; he was the son of a north of England policeman of Irish descent, and was a young journalist on the *Newcastle Daily Chronicle*. This was J. L. Garvin. In him poetry- and music-enthusiasm was like a genius in itself;

he became sublimated into the poetry he read or recited from his marvellous memory. And Thompson was to benefit by his tempestuous adoption, for Garvin's public testimony to him was not only early but pre-eminent; and there exists a letter concerning him, which Garvin wrote to Meynell, copied out by the poet, when it was shown him, in his own hand and preserved among his scanty treasures. A review of *Poems* had appeared in the *Newcastle Daily Chronicle*, so striking a one that Meynell wrote to the anonymous critic. It was Garvin's reply to Meynell which Thompson copied as a stirring message reaching him from an outer world.

12 Harrison Place, Newcastle-on-Tyne.
27th March 1894.

My dear Sir,

Pressure of work at the *Chronicle* & domestic trouble have conspired to delay my cordial acknowledgement of your courteous and generous letter about my review of Mr. Thompson's book. I do thank you for it sincerely. I know something of you and *Merry England* as well as of Mrs. Meynell's works, and that Mr. Thompson owes much to your intuition of his greatness. I value your praise in this connection more than any man's, and since I myself have still the undulled edge of a very young man's very vain appetite, your letter gave me more pleasure than you knew.

Indeed I do wish that I could claim your welcome at your house. Up in the north here if one has a passion for the finer letters one must possess his insulated soul in much patience. My only brother who was twin with me in taste went away to the Cape three weeks ago to escape phthisis and so I have now a quite solitary mind, owing to which all my literary criticism has such an essential egoism that I never know myself whether it is really sound or helpful to my readers or not, though I have been bound to write it that way. You do not understand even yet why your letter pleased me so much.

Four years ago an Ushaw man spoke of a Francis Thompson who had been or then was at Ushaw and wrote poems like Shelley. I had never heard of Mr. Thompson & the great comparison gave me at once the meanest opinion of my Ushaw friend's taste.

But at the beginning of '92 I came across the number of *Merry England* containing "The Making of Viola." Now I cannot tell you what I think of the angelic ingenuousness of that poem: it exercised over me an instant fascination from which I never shall escape; and though I never heard of him again until his volume was announced I was prepared to find that he had a most sweet and singular note, though not of course for the scope & sublimity of mind which the *Poems* disclosed. As it happened Mathews and Lane did not send me a copy for review; later I sent for a copy of the second edition. In the meantime my brother had borrowed a copy and went Thompson-mad. He declaimed the "Hound of Heaven" to me even while I wrote political "leaders." Still I was obdurate and a little irritated when these "snatches of Uranian antiphon" broke grandly through my own comments upon the Russo-German commercial treaty or Professor Garner's theories about the garrulous gorilla; in short I rebelled against the greatness of Mr. Thompson's own work.

Then I opened the book myself and read it right through. Then I began at the first page again and went on to the last. Then I read "Manus Animam Pinxit," "Her Portrait" and "To my Godchild" until I knew them by heart; the poems began to swarm in my head like bees. And then I wrote the review. I am glad you liked it.

I was in London two days before you wrote your letter, my brother having sailed from Southampton. I rarely go there, but I shall hope to see you in the autumn. Last July Mr. T. P. O'Connor invited me to join the staff of the *Evening Sun* as leader-writer but I refused; and shall not attempt to go to London for a few years when I have a much more efficiently equipped mind than now. Perhaps I may hope to have some news of Mr. Thompson from you from time to time; and I shall not always inflict such a world without end reply upon you. I thank you again for your cordial and encouraging appreciation & beg you to believe me

Yours very faithfully,
J. Louis Garvin

It was of course with Meynell rather than with Thompson himself that Garvin formed a personal tie when, in the autumn of that year, 1894, he came to Palace Court. Meynell was the most accessible of men, Thompson the least. In the tremendous industry of the journalistic position he acquired in London, Garvin was often lost to his friends, but he and Meynell had an undying appreciation of each other's qualities. Garvin called Meynell "the born smoother of ways." He wrote to him after many years in 1922: "I forget nothing, nothing, nothing; and even the little things you say and do with grace of heart unknown to yourself never escape me, never."

But Garvin, in a few characteristic letters to Thompson, as the years went by, kept alive the spark of their communication. In 1897 a "Jubilee Ode" by Thompson appeared in the *Manchester Guardian*, which Garvin, writing to Thompson, compared with that of the poet laureate, Alfred Austin. "Hot Jacobite as I am for England's one legitimate laureate by native grace & right divine, I could not repress the movement of natural pity for the respectable & conscientious wearer of statutory bays, who tries so hard to fly as if *The Times* page were Salisbury Downs & he a bustard. Every flap a stanza; thirty flaps of the most desperate volatile intention; & no forrarder to the empyrean,—where the Thompson ode sails with one supreme dominion through the azure depths of air—vital, radiant, lovely." And writing again that year about an article on Browning, Garvin comments on his own habit of absorption in any one of his "poets of the moment": "Tell me by what native instinct or faculty acquired you so easily avoid henotheism in your critical writings. My poet of the moment, as I am drawn to his centre & become enveloped in his light, seems to absorb all the radiance of all song. I know there are exterior suns, but the poet only remembered bears up with difficulty against him immediately contemplated. It is henotheism exactly. But here you take the crabbed case of Browning, you extricate him from the multitude of words & you directly declare middle justice upon him, & so he betakes him to his place."

In the *Bookman* of March, 1897, Garvin's fervour about Thompson's first two volumes would need to be remembered when *New Poems* in that same year was widely condemned and remained unsold.

We do not think we forget any of the splendid things of an English anthology when we say that the "Hound of Heaven" seems to us on the whole the most wonderful lyric in the language. It fingers all the stops of the spirit, and we hear now a thrilling and dolorous note of doom and now the quiring of the spheres and now the very pipes of Pan, but, under all, the still sad music of humanity. It is the return of the nineteenth century to Thomas à Kempis. . . . Mr. Thompson's poetry scarcely comes by way of the outward eye at all. He scarcely depends upon occasions. In a dungeon one imagines that he would be no less a poet. The regal air, the prophetic ardours, the apocalyptic vision, the supreme utterance—he has them all. A rarer, more intense, more strictly predestinate genius has never been known to poetry.

But the man whom Thompson was to know in a more whole way and in a kinship which neither would have found in hundreds of years in any other, was Coventry Patmore. Patmore's poetry was first in order of time, and it was easy to find a resemblance in Thompson's. (Arthur Symons saw in *Poems* a "close imitation of Mr. Patmore and Crashaw.") But it was also easy to know otherwise. In respect of metre Thompson agreed that his odes were "based on the principles which Mr. Patmore may virtually be said to have discovered." The irregular metre of his *Unknown Eros* Patmore himself described as one in which the length of line was controlled by its emotional significance. Thompson similarly refers in one of his notebooks to "temporal variations of metre responsive to ye emotions, like ye fluctuations of human respiration, which also varies indefinitely under the passage of changeful emotions, and yet keeps an approximate temporal uniformity." But Thompson could not accept indiscriminate generalization as to a resemblance. He commented in a letter to Meynell on one of his critics: "Of course he is right about ye 'To Monica Thought Dying,' but that & one or two other poems are not sufficient on which to base a charge of making Mr. Patmore a model. It would have been well, indeed, for ye restraint & sanity of ye poems if I *had* submitted somewhat to ye influence of Mr. Patmore's example." There could however be an unconscious plagiarism: Thompson's "For Spring leaps in the Womb of the Year" in *Sister Songs* had, he discovered, a parallel in Patmore's

> O, Baby Spring,
> That flutter'st sudden 'neath the breast of Earth
> A month before the birth.

Thompson would have cancelled his own line but "finding I could not disengage it," he wrote in his Preface, "without injury to the passage in which it is embedded, I have preferred to leave it, with this acknowledgement to a poet rich enough to lend to the poor."

Patmore, on the subject of their similarity, later wrote to Thompson: "Two readings leave your Poem [*Sister Songs*] very obscure in parts, but not, perhaps, more obscure than *prophecy* should be. I see, with joy, how nearly we are upon the same lines, but our visions could not be true were they quite the same; and no one can really see anything but his own vision. In the manner of your verse you are gaining in simplicity, which is a great thing. In the matter, I think, you outstrip me. I am too concrete and intelligible. I fear greatly lest what I have written may do more harm than good by exposing divine realities to profane apprehension, and by inflaming 'popular esotericism.' " He repeated on another occasion: "I am not sure you may not be a greater poet than I am."

As the close friend of the Meynells, Patmore had naturally identified himself from the outset with any interest so intense as theirs in Thompson's powers as they first became known; and, often generously sharing their tasks, he had joined in the reading of the proofs of *Poems* in 1893, and he had met Thompson at Palace Court later in that same year. Writing about *Poems* in the

Fortnightly in July he was still largely interested in him in the Meynell connection—in a very long sentence indeed.

A singular and very interesting history will convince thousands whom the rumour of it may reach, that he is an "extraordinary person"; the heroic faith in and devotion to the interests of his genius which, through long years, has been shown by at least two friends, one of them a lady not inferior in genius to his own; his recognition of her helpfulness by a series of poems which St. John of the Cross might have addressed to St. Theresa, and which, had she not established by her own writings a firm and original hold on fame, would have carried her name to posterity in company with that of "Mrs. Ann Killigrew"; the very defects of his writing, which will render manifest, by contrast, its beauties, thereby ingratiating "the crowd incapable of perfectness"; his abundant and often unnecessary obscurities, which will help his popularity, as Browning's did his, by ministering to the vanity of such as profess to be able to see through mill-stones, are all circumstances which will probably do more for his immediate acceptance by the literary public than qualities which ought to place him, even should he do no more than he has done, in the permanent ranks of fame, with Cowley and with Crashaw.

Commenting to Alice Meynell on the whole *Fortnightly* article, which he had not immediately seen, Thompson wrote from Pantasaph:

Had I written upon the evidence of the extract in the *Register*, I should have pronounced Mr. Patmore's article magnificently generous. And that, read between the lines, would have meant that I thought Mr. Patmore had let generosity overmaster justice. But the complete article makes quite another impression. I am delighted with it. From first to last it is pre-eminently *just*; and manages to combine fine praise with discriminate and illuminating criticism of defects and limitations. "Illuminating"; for other critics note the symptoms of one's poetic maladies, he diagnoses the seat of disease. I have got more help and self-knowledge from his article than from anything else which has appeared. Will you convey to him my warmest thanks for an article which cannot but remain a landmark in my life? I feel that my thanks will acquire a grace not their own, by being delivered to him through you.

But though Patmore and Thompson might start their intercourse as two branches of a Meynell tree, their unity almost immediately took them far beyond that connection. In regard to Alice Meynell's self-contained, or family-contained, existence, both men were in outer darkness—in Thompson's case the unquestioned natural darkness of night; in Patmore's the blackness of despair and doom. What Patmore sought from her in this last distraught grief of his life is undefined. He may have thought that in her marriage there could not be full communion in what was to him her rare genius. It was not unnatural to think of her separately from those close about her. She was distinct, as a person of creative genius must be—bound to be solitary in her creative life. Certainly Patmore did not link her entirely and exclusively with her husband, nor include him in any special degree of interest. He did not realize that though her powers were far beyond her husband's she was united to him in an equality in which it cannot be said which gave and which received the most. Neither did George Meredith, any more than Patmore, when he became her great admirer, imagine her so indivisibly partnered as to extend to Meynell his particular friendship. In both cases Meynell would have no thought of its being otherwise. Of Patmore, Thompson and Meredith, it was Thompson who loved both.

Patmore was at the same time the last person to wish to ignore or injure a marriage-tie. But somewhere, beside her marriage and above all else in her life, he thought a place was his. Her exceeding love of his poetry made it seem certain. But this conception of his may have been one not quite realizable in any human relation; it was not realizable with her. "Now I have lost the great friendship of my life," Patmore wrote to Thompson at Pantasaph, "I value yours above all others." "Though my physical health is pretty well restored," he wrote in 1895, "I go on with a perpetual heartache. None can see God—or goddess—and live. . . . I have only seen our Friend twice during the past ten months." And in the same year: "It is always a great thing to me to receive a letter from you. My heart goes forth to you as it goes to no other man; for are we not singularly visited by a great common delight and a great common sorrow? Is not this to be one in Christ?"

But before this, from their first awareness of each other in 1893, there had been the consciousness of a rare affinity. Patmore, as a member of the Third Order of St. Francis, had been on a visit to the Pantasaph monastery. Thompson then wrote to Alice Meynell: "I have had a charming visit from Mr. Patmore. He bore himself towards me with a dignity & magnanimity which are not of this age's stature." And remembering the occasion later: "Though never a word on either side directly touched or explained the exceptional nature of the proposal, it was well understood between us—by me no less than by him—that it was no common or conventional friendship he asked of me. Not therefore had he sought out my Welsh hermitage, & scalpelled ye fibres of me." Patmore wrote home: "Francis Thompson and all the Fathers spent two hours last night in my room, and we had excellent talk. Father Anselm, the Superior, and a profound contemplative, said he had never read anything so fine as the 'Precursor.'" So for Patmore at any rate Thompson could talk. He wrote to Patmore: "You are the only man with whom I can talk at all. With all others it is a matter of playing an intermittent chord or so, as an accompaniment to *their* talk. . . . Yours is the conversation of a man who has trodden before me the way which for years I trod. . . ." And an entry in his notebook describes Patmore's talk and the effect on himself as "companion." "Then he would open out & reveal—not merely information, nor merely brilliance,—but a whole vast philosophy of life & ye universe he revealed in spacious meditated sentences, which descended like a cloud of light. A helpless talker in society, his companion [himself], in the amity of a man like this, caught up his fellow's deep utterances & pursued with an after-train of illuminative corroboration." But unless they were alone not even Patmore could confer a gift of speech on Thompson. Alice Meynell, when he went with her to stay with the Patmores at Lymington, noticed how during drives Thompson sat silent, his eyes fixed on the floor of the carriage with a harrowing expression on his face.

Thompson might also have said to Patmore: "You are the only man with whom I can correspond." During the two years of their intimacy they may not have written often but Thompson wrote to Patmore as he wrote to no one else. He could not do otherwise in contact with the man of whom he wrote in his notebook: "What I put forth as a bud he blew on and it blossomed. The contact of our ideas was dynamic; he reverberated my idea with such and so many echoes that it returned to me greater than I gave it forth. He opened it as you open an oyster, or placed it under a miscroscope, and showed me what it contained." Also, in their letters each was the sole confidant of each in that "great common delight and great common sorrow" with which they were "singularly visited." There they were interrelated. "I am sorry to think," Thompson wrote once, "that the outpouring of my own bitter mood possibly stimulated yours; when I should rather do what I can to mitigate the darkness of your life."

Their similarity in thought made it necessary to defend, even between one another, more possible suspicion of plagiarism. Thompson wrote from Pantasaph in the summer of 1895 in sending his "Orient Ode":

Dear Mr. Patmore,

I send you this . . . not for its literary merit, but because without such a disclaimer I fear you would think I had been the first to find your book [*Religio Poetae*] "d——d good to steal from." As a matter of fact it was written soon after Easter, & was suggested by passages in ye liturgies of Holy Saturday, some of which—at rather appalling length—I have quoted at the head of its two parts. That was done for the sake of those who might cavil at its doctrines. Indeed—with superfluous caution—I intended much of it to be sealed; but your book has mainly broken the seals I had put upon it. There is quite enough in it of yours, without the additional presumption that I had hastened to make immediate use of your last book.

As far as others are concerned it must rest under that imputation to which the frequent coincidence in the selection of symbolism—as an example, the basing of a whole passage on the symbolic meaning of the *West*—very naturally leads. To yourself such coincidence is explicable, it will not be to outsiders.

Yours always,
Francis Thompson

He next writes: ". . . I want to allude particularly to your invaluable correction of my misuse of ye Western symbolism. . . . I asked myself how it came that we reckoned our points of the compass facing to ye North. The only explanation I could surmise was that it was a relic of Set-worship among our Saxon ancestors. Do you mean that *historically* men have prayed in three distinct periods to W., E., & N. ?" Patmore replied: "The world has worshipped turning to the West, to the East, and to the North. The 'New Eve' is the South, and, when we turn thither, all things will be renewed, and God will 'turn our captivity as Rivers in the South,' and we shall know Him in the flesh 'from sea to sea.' " A month later Patmore still dwells on this subject:

I wish I could see and talk to you on the subject of the symbolism you speak of. The Bible and all the theologies are full of it, but it is too deep and significant to get itself uttered in writing. The Psalms especially are full of it. On the matter of the "North" note that verse: "Promotion cometh not from the South, nor the East, nor the West." That is, it cometh from the North. The North seems always to signify the original Godhead, the "Father"—or the devil. For the same symbol is used in the Bible and the mythologies for either extreme. "Water," for example, is constantly used for the sensible nature in its extreme purity, as in the Blessed Virgin, or in its extreme corruption. This honouring of the "North" may very likely have been at the bottom of the seeking of the points of the compass from that quarter.

I hope some day to see and have speech with you on this and other matters. Meantime I will only hint that the North represents the simple Divine virility, the South the Divine womanhood, the East their synthesis in the Holy Spirit, and the West the pure natural womanhood "full of grace." I could give you no end of proofs, but it would take me months to collect them, from all I have read and forgotten.

Thompson replied:

Creccas Cottage, Pantasaph, Wednesday [1895].
Dear Mr. Patmore,

I have been intending to write to you since your letter regarding the symbolism of the points of the compass; but ill-health and depression have delayed me. A violent paroxysm of the A. M.-malady burst on me at the time I wrote *A Captain of Song* (hence the tone of that poem); such as I have not known since the days, three years ago, when I put my passion under my feet. It has only recently dropped from me, and left me feeling broken and much older. Indeed, one woman here told me that my beard was showing more white streaks, and my manner growing sterner. Your own experience, I think, will make you pardon my negligence.

I think your *Saturday* letter very felicitously put. But alas! small are the chances of any government acting on it. I fear the "compliment to Journalism" points too surely to Edwin Arnold.[1]

I have not received the *Selections*.[2] A. M. has only once in my life sent me any book of hers—her *Essays*—and I expect it is the only one I ever shall receive from her. Women—and this sweet Lady and fine genius is "no more but even a woman"— have a fatal ease in "getting used" to devotion. It soon comes to seem no such mighty merit on your part; since after all it is not your doing—you cannot help it. I should indeed like to see the book. The selections in themselves must possess a peculiar interest for me; and the Preface I am most eager to read.

[1] Patmore had written a letter to the *Saturday Review* advocating the appointment of Alice Meynell as poet laureate. Later, when Alfred Austin was appointed, Thompson further commented to Patmore: "What a pity you could not have upheld the dignity of the Laureateship in the eyes of Europe! This absurd appointment might have been pointedly contrived to give the office its death-blow. What man of mark will take it when Austin is gathered to the kindred shades of Nahum Tate, Whitehead and Pye?"

[2] *The Poetry of Pathos and Delight*. Passages selected by Alice Meynell from the works of Patmore. Heinemann, 1896.

You rather mistook the purport of my inquiry in regard to the symbolic question. I wanted to know whether there had been any actual progressive development among the nations with regard to the quarters in which they worshipped—as an historic fact, apart from symbolic meaning. But this is such a minor matter, and the concluding hint of your letter contains so much of value to me, that I am not sorry you misapprehended me. Of course I am quite aware that it is impossible to answer openly—indeed impossible to ask openly—deeper matters in a letter. But that is not requisite in my case. It is enough that my gaze should be set in the necessary direction; the rest may safely be left to the practised fixity of my looking. Indicative language, such as you employed in your letter, you may safely trust me to understand. With regard to what you say about the symbolism of the North, I had substantially discerned it for myself. Indeed it formed part of a little essay which I had projected, arising out of a footnote to an essay already written. It will be none the worse for the corroboration of your remarks: there is always something in your way of stating even what is already to me a *res visa*, which adds sight to my seeing. The quotation from the Psalms is new and grateful to me. But I was aware of the thing to which it points. Shakespeare speaks of—

"The lordly monarch of the north;"

(I was confusing it with a passage in Comus); and Butler remarks—

"Cardan believed great states depend
Upon the tip o' th' Bear's tail's end."

Set was given by the Egyptians the lordship of temporal powers; and to him the Bear was sacred. And of course I am aware of the esoteric meaning of this and of Cardan's saying. Indeed this was what I intended by my observation, that I surmised our Northern aspect in reckoning the compass to be a relic of Set-worship among our Teuton ancestors; though of course I was aware that Set, by that name, was an Egyptian deity. Also I am familiar with the principle of dual significance in this and mythological imagery generally. Indeed, without the knowledge of this principle, both Scripture and the mythologies are full of baffling contradictions. When I began seriously to consider mythologies comparatively I cut myself with the broken reed on which all the "scientific" students fall back—this significance belongs to an earlier, that to a later period of development. But having eyes, which "scientific" students have not, I soon saw that facts gave me the lie in all directions. And when I came to make a comprehensive study of the Hebrew prophets, with the Eastern mythologies in mind, I speedily discerned the systematic use of the dual significance, and difficulty vanished.

I encountered one of the local ghosts the other day, for the first time in my now considerable residence here. I will tell you of him when I am in better spirits. It is a suicidal day, warm and wet, with a filthy standing fog.

Always yours,
Francis Thompson

Patmore replied:

Thank you for your very interesting letter, which shows me how extraordinarily alike are our methods of and experience in contemplation. . . . God bless and help you to bear your crown of thorns, and to prosper in the great, though possibly obscure, career He seems to have marked out for you! My work, such as it is, is done, and I am now only waiting, somewhat impatiently, for death, and the fulfilment of the promises of God, which include all that we have ever desired here, in perfection beyond all hope.

Yours,
C. P.

In March, 1896, Patmore wrote to Pantasaph:

Lymington, Hants.

I am very sorry to hear continued bad news of you. I cannot give much better of myself. In fact, I am literally dying of having seen God, and of the vision having been withdrawn. I have been continually ill—very ill—for some two years. Two eminent Doctors have asked me whether this long series of acute maladies was preceded by some long sorrow! My only comfort is that the end cannot be far off.

The end was not far off, but four months later, and four months before his death, he wrote after Thompson had been for a month's visit to London:

My dear Thompson,   Lymington. July 29, '96.

You were looking so unwell when we parted that, not having yet heard from you, I am somewhat alarmed. Pray let me have a post-card.

If at any time you find yourself seriously ill, and do not find the attendance, food, etc., sufficiently good, tell me and I will go to Pantasaph to take care of you for any time you might find me useful. It would be a great pleasure and honour to serve you in any way.

Yours ever,
Coventry Patmore

But Thompson replied:

I thank you for the great honour you have done me by your offer to come up and look after me if I needed nursing. Fortunately it has not come to that yet.

Patmore died in November. The news coming to Pantasaph made Thompson a bereft and lonely man. "There has passed away the greatest genius of the century," he wrote to Mrs. Patmore at Lymington, "& from me a friend whose like I shall not see again; one so close to my own soul that ye distance of years between us was hardly felt, nor could ye distance of miles separate us. . . . The irrevocableness of such a grief is mocked by many words; these few words least wrong it. My friend is dead, & I had but one such friend." To Meynell he wrote: "Of nothing can I write just now. You know what friends we had been these last two years. I heard from him but ye Monday before his death. There is no more to say, because there is too much to say."

In his private notebook he spoke solitary words of greater implication. "It remains a personal (& wonderful) memory that to me sometimes, athwart ye shifting clouds of converse, was revealed by glimpses the direct vision of that oceanic vast.of intellect." To Thompson the greatness of Patmore's prose and poetry was only less than the greatness of Patmore himself.

113

In another note he writes: "Age alone will grasp in some dim measure what must have been the unmanifested powers of a mind from which could go forth this starry manifestation; and what 'silence full of wonders' interspaced his opulent frugality of speech."

It was now that Thompson left Pantasaph for London. He had need of what other human resources he possessed, and these lay only in Wilfrid Meynell and his family. He returned to the wing of a man with whom he spoke a different language from that used to Patmore, largely one of explanations and excuses and sufferings. "Of course my identification of ye disease from which I suffered last spring but one with *beri-beri* (devoutly though I hold it) may be quite wrong without affecting ye practical point in the least. The undoubted fact is that 'twas a deadly disease caused originally by malnutrition." "I am upset with a bad cold and rheumatism in ye knees, so that I clump down stairs of mornings like ye elephant who

has knees
But none for bending."

"I intended to call in tonight, but was taken sick at ye critical moment"—a constant cry, this, as repetitive as the dismal days of ill-health themselves; a needy cry too: "I send you my lodging account." "My landlady is urgent with me to remind you about her bill." This was the obverse side of the Thompson who wrote to Patmore. It was daily small-talk to the man who provided the hearth and home which life needs too, and is thankful for. Their tie survived the testing condition of a day-by-day relationship, of struggling circumstances, and of the provocation of one man's practical ascendancy over another. It afforded Thompson the luxury of a rare grumble at some arrangement not to his mind. For Meynell's habit of being right in many things and for many people was fortified by a strain of obstinacy; and Thompson must sometimes have felt chivvied by a will stronger than his own. But their association was of permanent life-giving value to each of them; and it is possible to think that no other man alive would have filled the part, in an all-round way, of Thompson's unusual requirements as Wilfrid Meynell filled it by being himself.

VIII

THOMPSON'S coat is well remembered on fire in the cupboard of the room where he slept at Palace Court, from a pipe alight in the pocket. In 1897, the first year of his return to London, there came to Meynell one night—it was on the 25th of November—a Metropolitan Police telegraphic message. "*Please inform Mr. Wilfred Meynell no. 47 Palace Court Bayswater Hill that at 7.10 pm 25th inst Francis Thomason was knocked down by a H.C. at High Holborn and is now detained at the Homeopathic Hospital Queens Square suffering from cut head. Will he attend. Reply.*" H.C. was hansom cab. Writing, for the first time for years, to his sister who was a nun—a letter which he forgot ever to post—Thompson said:

> . . . Thereon forthwith followed ye severe & most unhappy cab accident. I have had a year of disasters. You will notice a new address [39 Goldney Road, Harrow Road, N.W.] at the head of this letter. I have been burned out of my former lodgings. The curtain caught fire just after I had got into bed, & I upset ye lamp in trying to extinguish it. My hands were badly blistered, & I sustained a dreadful shock, besides having to walk ye streets all night. The room was quite burned out.

A retrospective glimpse of Thompson at Goldney Road is contained in a letter addressed to the B.B.C. in 1951 after a broadcast on the poet.

> 15 Belmont Road, Beckenham, Kent.
> 10/12/51.

> On Sunday evening 9/12/51 I listened to the latter part of the programme on Francis Thompson. You gave the district, but perhaps you were not aware the address was 39 Goldney Road, Paddington.

My mother, Mrs. A. Frey, was the landlady, and owner of the house and died there in 1924.

Mr. Thompson's room was on a level with the front door, at the back of the house. I remember when I used to pass his door, which had a glass panel with a red margin, with cut glass corners, I used to hear him saying Oh God, Oh God. I went to Canada in May 1903, but I remember my younger brother wrote me in 1908 that he had died, and sent newspaper cuttings about it.

Yours sincerely,
L. Frey.

P.S. I remember a lady and gent brought a suit of clothes for him it was a brownish mixture in colour. I often saw him walking towards Westbourne Grove, and just had to follow him, because he would cross the road amongst traffic as in a dream, it was a marvel he wasn't killed.

L. H. F.

His lodgings, never very far from Harrow Road, were often changed; his landladies found his ways at best inconvenient; they were a kind race. One of them, when Everard Meynell saw her, regretted that Thompson did not avail himself of companionship downstairs. "Many a time I've asked him to have his bit of lunch in with me and the other 'mental'—oh yes, she's a mental case, as I may have told you." Another landlady showed where he had worn a threadbare circle in her carpet pacing round the table in the night till bed-time in the morning. For ten years from 1897 he was to emerge from those dingy respectable doors mostly to make his way to Palace Court or to deliver copy at the offices of the weeklies for which he wrote, his caped ulster hanging more and more loosely on him as the years passed. What unconsoled physical distress was known inside those lodging-house walls is revealed in stray undated entries in his notebooks.

The other night (after work against time which belated my dinner till past eleven) I went to bed fordone, dripping with cold, quivering at ye icy sheets, mashed & writhen with cramp, so that I had to get up every quarter of an hour & walk about, to rid myself of ye gnarled & wringing pain. I could have cried

KATIE KING

COVENTRY PATMORE

with Caliban: "I am not Thompson, but a cramp!" Sleep was impossible till towards six or seven of ye morning, when I subsided into broken & uneasy slumber. I felt as if I could hold on ye struggle no further, but must give way through sheer outspent body.

But when he arrived from Pantasaph—in good shape for him —in the last month of 1896 he stayed for a while at Palace Court, and from there he even went for two short stays with Mr. and Mrs. Doubleday at Westminster, friends of the Meynells, Doubleday being a partner in Constable's, the firm which was to replace Lane as publishers of Thompson's *New Poems*. For visiting, Meynell had equipped him with what must have been a decided misfit—a loan from a fairly broad man to a very narrow one.

> 2 Whitehall Gardens, S.W.
> 17 December 1896.

Dear Wilfrid,
  I reached here all right last night, & found that they had put off dinner till eight o'clock, so that I was in plenty of time. I have done a perhaps rash thing—promised Doubleday to come to him again when they return after Xmas. I forgot that you cannot be without your dress-clothes continuously—particularly at a time when you are likely often to have occasion for them. They dress for dinner here, so that I shall have to use them daily.
  Mrs. Doubleday is very kind; & she is a simply exquisite pianist. Doubleday and I fraternized over music. It seems quiet and nice enough so far; I am left to my own devices during the day, which is just what I like.

> Always yours,
> Francis Thompson

At Palace Court things were busy and active. There were other habitual callers, two almost as daily or nightly as Thompson himself when he had removed to his lodgings. Meals were re-served for the latecomer. It was not a very ordered household. Alice Meynell relied on servants with an inborn trust. When some inadequacy became blatant it was the master of the house who took a sudden fit of enjoyable house-cleaning, and made use of some convinced method of his own of mopping and flicking, with the children commandeered to help. The fact that the habitual visitors might equally find him immersed in house-maiding or in writing a brochure on Cardinal Newman made the casual unconstraint which he always created about him ; the intimates knew they came to a place of business, whatever the kind; they could be surprised at nothing. The house was built round an outdoor shaft or well, which lit the windows which gave on to it. At intervals Meynell considered it a hygienic necessity to throw dozens of bucketfuls of water from the topmost windows down this deep well occupying the middle of the house. It was a wet and hilarious task performed with great energy, and approved by the children. After it the whole house smelt of wetness, like the world after a thunder shower. Food was relatively good or bad according to the cook of the moment; there was far too little food-consciousness in the house at that time for it to reach visitor-standards. Some of them in subsequent memoirs have made tolerant but unanimous reference to deficiencies. Even Thompson must have achieved some modest tea-shop or eating-house standard dear to him, for on one occasion he remarked with tremulous discontent: "Wilfrid, the Palace Court food is *shocking*."

"Give my love to Monica," or as a variant "my love to Monicella"; "my love to Cuckoo & to all the chicks"; those messages which had come unfailingly from Thompson at Pantasaph were written with feeling and longing. And now he was back among the children to whom he had best spoken his love in the poems addressed to them. He was moved to happiness at the thought that children took to him. He tells in a letter written in 1900 how having got involved in Coronation-night celebrations in the streets some children had teased and played with him, one coming so close that he could put his hand in to her "bright tresses." He adds: "You see I retain my old slavery to childhood; though this is the first time I knew that I retained anything of my old attraction for children, which I thought I had quite lost, having got too old & black of visage." That his friendly relation with children amounted to his having an attraction for them was perhaps the exaggeration of a man too much deprived of personal ties; he was not the visitor at the sound of whose special knock the Palace Court children raced down the stairs to be the first to open the door; he is not remembered as ever being sought by them or causing the smallest stir of that expectation which children easily feel. But they were never afraid or strange with him, and a child would hold his hand as naturally as hold her doll. They found him easily gullible. When he went with the family to Friston in Suffolk for a summer holiday, and with difficulty put on the children's stockings for them after they had paddled, it was easy to make him believe that there was a right and a left foot for a stocking, and that he had put them on wrong. The Meynells had made him godfather to a son born in 1891. "I am utterly unable to express to you what I feel regarding it," he wrote. He could hardly have expressed it more. In "To My Godchild" he imagines the child a future poet blossoming from his dust.

> And when, immortal mortal, droops your head,
> And you, the child of deathless song, are dead;
> Then, as you search with unaccustomed glance
> The ranks of Paradise for my countenance,
> Turn not your tread along the Uranian sod
> Among the bearded counsellors of God:
> For if in Eden as on earth are we,
> I sure shall keep a younger company:
> Pass where beneath their rangèd gonfalons
> The starry cohorts shake their shielded suns,
> The dreadful mass of their enridgèd spears;
> Pass where majestical the eternal peers,
> The stately choice of the great Saintdom, meet—
> A silvern segregation, globed complete
> In sandalled shadow of the Triune feet;
> Pass by where wait, young poet-wayfarer,
> Your cousined clusters, emulous to share
> With you the roseal lightnings burning 'mid their hair;
> Pass the crystalline sea, the Lampads seven:—
> Look for me in the nurseries of Heaven.

At Storrington the child "Daisy" had captivated him.

Her beauty smoothed earth's furrowed face.
  She gave me tokens three:—
A look, a word of her winsome mouth,
  And a wild raspberry.

A berry red, a guileless look,
  A still word,—strings of sand!
And yet they made my wild, wild heart
  Fly down to her little hand.

For standing artless as the air,
  And candid as the skies,
She took the berries with her hand,
  And the love with her sweet eyes. . . .

When Thompson was at Friston with the Meynells for a summer holiday, a simple favour bestowed on him by Monica drove into him, because he was all sensibility about the child, the full pained consciousness of what it was to be himself—and the triumph too. She had picked a poppy and given it into his hand, telling him to keep it always; and in this flower of sleep he saw his own image.

The sleep-flower sways in the wheat its head,
Heavy with dreams as that with bread:
The goodly grain and the sun-flushed sleeper
The reaper reaps, and Time the reaper.

I hang 'mid men my needless head,
And my fruit is dreams, as theirs is bread:
The goodly men and the sun-hazed sleeper
Time shall reap, but after the reaper
The world shall glean of me, me the sleeper.

Love, love! your flower of withered dream
In leavèd rhyme lies safe, I deem,
Sheltered and shut in a nook of rhyme,
From the reaper man, and his reaper Time.

Love! *I* fall into the claws of Time:
But lasts within a leavèd rhyme
All that the world of me esteems—
My withered dreams, my withered dreams.

As time passed the children became school-children. They were unwilling for the school-friends who came home with them to see the unordinary figure who haunted the house.

The year 1897 was one of active journalism for Thompson. Charles Lewis Hind, the editor of the *Academy*, welcomed weekly contributions from him, and both editor and staff tolerated his unpunctuality for the sake of what he could produce. Wilfrid Whitten, the assistant editor, wrote:

We gave Thompson as many books of theology, history, biography and of course poetry as he cared to review. It was a usual thing, in reading the proofs, for one of us to exclaim aloud on his splendid handling of a subject demanding the best literary knowledge and insight. . . . In talk on great subjects he was slow or silent; on trifles he became grotesquely tedious. This dreamer seemed to be surprised into a kind of exhilaration at finding himself in contact with small realities. And then the fountains of memory would be broken up, or some quaint corner of his *amour propre* would be touched. He would explain nine times what was clear, and talk about snuff and indigestion or the posting of a letter until the room swam round us. A stranger figure than Thompson's was not to be seen in London. Gentle in looks, half wild in externals, his face worn by pain and the fierce reactions of laudanum, his hair and straggling beard neglected, he had yet a distinction and an aloofness of bearing that marked him in the crowd. A clearer mind, a more naïvely courteous manner, were not to be found. His great brown cape, which he would wear on the hottest days, his disastrous hat, and his dozen neglects and make-shifts, were only the insignia of our "Francis" and of the ripest literary talent on the paper. No money (and in his later years Thompson suffered more from the possession of money than from the lack of it) could keep him in a decent suit of clothes for long. Yet he was never "seedy." From a newness too dazzling to last, and seldom achieved at that, he passed at once into a picturesque nondescript garb that was all his own and made him resemble some weird pedlar or packman in an etching by Ostade. This impression of him was helped by the fish-basket which he wore slung round his shoulders by a strap. It had occurred to him that such a basket would be a convenient receptacle for the books which he took away for review, and he added this touch to an outward appearance which already detached him from millions. . . . He had ceased to make demands on life. He earmarked nothing for his own. As a reviewer, enjoying the run of the office, he never pounced on a book; he waited, and he accepted. Interested still in life, he was no longer intrigued by it. He was free from both apathy and desire. Unembittered, he kept his sweetness and sanity, his dewy laughter, and his fluttering gratitude. In such a man outward ruin could never be pitiable or ridiculous, and indeed he never bowed his noble head but in adoration. I think the secret of his strength was this: that he had cast up his accounts with God and man, and thereafter stood in the mud of earth with a heart wrapped in such a fire as touched Isaiah's lips.

Though many of the most interesting books of the time were given to Thompson for review, being no keeper he retained none. On one occasion he had to apologize to the *Academy* editor for inadvertently selling a book before he had reviewed it, and he tells him to dock him of the price of it.

> The only alternative [he writes] is for me to pick oakum (if they do that in debtors' gaols). And I have not ye talent for oakum-picking. Though I enjoyed ye distinguished tuition of a burglar, who had gone through many trials—and hours— in ye pursuit of this little-known art, I showed such mediocre capacity that ye Master did not encourage me to persevere. Besides, seeing how over-crowded ye profession is, it would be a pity for me to take ye oakum out of another man's fingers.

Late copy was more earnestly accounted for by such letters as this:

Dear Hind,

I muddled up ye time altogether. How, I do not understand. I started off soon after 2. Thinking I had time for a letter to ye *Academy* which it had been in my mind to write, I delayed my journey to write it. When I was drawing to a conclusion, I heard ye clock strike 3 (as it seemed to me). I thought I should soon be finished, so went on to the end. A few minutes later, as it appeared, ye clock struck again, & I counted 4. Alarmed, I rushed off—vexed that I should get in by half-past 4 instead of half-past 3, as I intended—& finished ye thing in ye train. I got to ye *Academy*, & was struck all of a heap. There was nobody there, & it was ten past six! How I did it, I do not even now understand. I will be with you in good time tomorrow. But that cannot make amends to myself for such a *fiasco* & waste of time.

Yours,
F. T.

Illness is the excuse time after time:

I was taken sick on my way to ye station, not having been to bed all night, & having been working a good part of today; & though I came on as soon as I could pull myself together again, I was too late. So I leave here ye Dumas article, which I brought with me & will bè down tomorrow morning.

The *Athenaeum* tried pretending the copy was needed a day early. Thompson realized it, and, always making good resolutions, adjured himself in a notebook: "Remember the new *Athenaeum* dodge testifies against you." About an article on "The Centenary Burns" a now-ageing W. E. Henley wrote: "Thompson's article, which came in this morning, is quite masterly throughout. The worst I can say against it is, indeed, that it anticipates some parts of my own terminal essay, so that I shall have to quote it instead of writing out of my own stomach." Towards the end of these years of journalism H. W. Massingham wrote, welcoming contributions: "I have always retained the utmost admiration for your poetic genius, and regard with much warmth its association with a paper like the *Nation*." In a notebook entry of later years

Thompson remarks in regard to this journalism: "Nevertheless, it is possible that (in those early days especially) I may have been debauched by the *Academy*. The editor demanded naked Truth, yet cried 'Decency!' when I exhibited her. Theoretically he cared nothing for what people might say; practically, if Mamma protested against ye disgraceful attack on Mr. Onlyson, he suggested that I had painted ye devil with a regrettable neglect of values."

How was London life panning out in inner experience, beneath this surface of industry, accidents and illness? The bedrock of him was poet, lover and spirit—and he was faring ill. He had come back to the proximity of Alice Meynell. His love in this woman's presence was more like someone else's love in absence; he would never be seen to look at her, and it was easier for him to write than speak to her. He entered in his notebook the summing-up of old and new experience.

I yielded to the insistent commands of my conscience and uprooted my heart—as I supposed. Later, the renewed presence of ye beloved lady renewed ye love I thought deracinated. For a while I swung vacillant. . . . I thought I owed it to her whom I loved more than my love of her finally to unroot that love, to pluck away the last fibres of it, that I might be beyond treachery to my resolved duty. And at this second effort I finished what ye first had left incomplete. The initial agony had really been decisive, and to complete the process needed only resolution. But it left that lady still ye first, ye one veritable, full-orbed & apocalyptic love of my life. Through her was shown me the uttermost of what love could be—the possible divinities and celestial prophecies of it. None other could have taught them quite thus, for none other had in her the like unconscious latencies of utter spirituality. Surely she will one day realise them, as by her sweet, humble, & stainless life she has deserved to do. . . .

It was experience behind a curtain, but one which in some exceptional conditions was still rent aside for her to see.

My own dear lady and mother,

How did it come about that what began between us in confidence this afternoon ended, somehow, in constraint & reticence? I could not understand it at ye time; I could only feel that, while I was tenderly grateful for your dear kindness, I had somehow fallen out of touch with you after ye first moment. And I was miserable to feel it. I have now come to ye conclusion that ye fault was all on my side. Though I said otherwise at lunch (for I hate parading one's private ills before strangers), I had slept little last night, eaten nothing in ye morning, and was able to eat little at lunch. So that I felt utterly spent, and unable to stand ye strain of emotion, or to respond to your spirit with ye instinctive perception I am accustomed to have for it. I trust you, honour you, & love you more than ever,—O believe me: it was simply that paralysis of ye heart & emotions which follows a prolonged strain upon them. Pardon me, & do not let it rest here. Confidence has gone too far not to go farther, or die altogether. Give me an opportunity tomorrow, if possible: at any rate ye sooner ye better. And I will open to you, if you wish it, my most secret soul; that on my side you may never misunderstand me through distrust or want of knowledge. That I promise you. On your side, be all exactly as you wish. It is marvellous to me how I missed grasping your sweet and sympathetic purpose this afternoon; but I did. Let it not persuade you to believe me anything but your loving child, friend, & sympathiser,

Francis

But never did these two meet on equal terms of emotion. So basic a difference in degree of feeling cannot achieve even minutes of complete unison; and any fluttering belief on Thompson's part that she was fully responsive to his "secret soul" lapsed into unsensational—even almost opportune—oblivion.

'Ninety-seven was the year in which the *New Poems* which Thompson had foretold would be his last book was savaged by the critics. "From ye higher standpoint I have gained, I think, in art & chastity of style," he had written to Meynell from Pantasaph when completing the book, "but have equally lost in fire and glow. 'Tis time that I was silent. This book carries me quite as far as my dwindling strength will allow; & if I wrote further in poetry, I should write down my own fame." Patmore had accepted the dedication when he was alive. "This should have been my second book," Thompson had written to him, "if W. M. had not frustrated my careful waiting by committing me to ye publication of my last ill-starred volume [*Sister Songs*]—which has sold only 349 copies in twelve months." The dedication still stood, and some of the poems were peculiarly Patmore's—"this strong sad soul of sovereign Song," as Thompson called him. "This latest, highest, of my work is now born dumb," he wrote. "It had been sung into his sole ears. Now there is none who speaks its language."

Of all the words one can wish unwritten, the scathing judgments by critics of a poet are the most painful if when read in retrospect they appear to have been uncalled-for—for one is reading them not with one's own eyes but with the poet's, who more likely than not was one of the hurt creatures of creation in any case. The instance of Thompson's *New Poems* may not be among the glaring ones of ill-judged abuse: faults of his condemned then may equally be disliked now. And much of the collection is hard reading.

> The first section exhibits mysticism in a limited and varying degree [Thompson wrote in a cancelled preface]. I feel my instrument yet too imperfect to profane by it the higher ranges. Much is transcendental rather than truly mystic. . . . Some of the poems are as much science as mysticism! but it is the science of the Future, not the science of the scientist. The "Orient Ode," on its scientific side, must wait at least fifty years for understanding. For there was never yet poet, beyond a certain range of insight, who could not have told the scientists what they will be teaching a hundred years hence. Science is a Caliban, only fit to hew wood and draw water for Prospero; and it is time Ariel were released from his imprisonment by the materialistic Sycorax.

He was aware of the challenge to disapproval. He wrote to Meynell: "I have put a whole section of ye lightest poems I ever wrote after ye first terribly trying section: to soothe ye critics' gums. . . . I have done what I could to lighten a very stern, sober, and difficult volume." So alienation in many critics was not unlikely, and yet it is painful to read the chorus now. "Nonsense-verses"; "barbarous jargon"; "a dictionary of obsolete English suffering from a fierce fit of delirium tremens"; " a terrible poem called 'An Anthem of Earth' without form and void, rhymeless and the work of a mediaeval and pedantic Walt Whitman"; those few out of many give an idea of Thompson's banishment into a further solitude than was his already. Critics are the public too. The book sold badly and was soon dead. The reading-thinking world must have seemed as desolately remote from him, with his transcendental themes and liturgical metaphor, as were the immediate physical incidents of the Edgware Road and other mean streets through which he was jostling his way daily and always alone.

What has to be wished unsaid is the abuse, for instance, of "The Mistress of Vision" (the "nonsense-verses"—which are in fact devoid of his faults); and indeed the solitary voice of Quiller-Couch even then affirmed: "I can only say that it recalls, after many days, the wonder and delight with which as a boy I first read 'Kubla Khan.' " And for another instance: the reception of his longest poem, "An Anthem of Earth," the "terrible poem"— which should have been called only difficult. These he saw condemned out of hand. From one of the few voices of approval— that of William Archer—he heard: "I assure you no conceivable reaction can wipe out or overlay such work as yours. It is firm based on the rock of absolute beauty; and this I say all the more confidently because it does not happen to appeal to my own speculative, or even my own literary, prejudices."

In Wilfrid Meynell there was one to whom Francis Thompson's work appealed without conditions; there seemed no end to its fitness for him nor his accordance with it—a fact which also contains an everlasting element of surprise. A man more of feeling than of intellect, with little literary erudition beyond what might be hastily improvised for the purpose of immediate journalism; author himself of much neat verse often turning on a punning play of words, he might not have been eligible for the almost-identification with Thompson which actually occurred. His young enamoured reading of the most-read of the poets had fallen into desuetude even more than happens with many. A list of the poets with whom he did not concern himself after youth would contain great names of all epochs, including Shakespeare. He was ardent but not scholarly. With the world of poetry he could not do otherwise than identify himself completely, and would not have thought that anyone could be more closely associated with it. Disapproving of a sketch made of him once by one of his daughters, he said: "That man has never read Keats." But the absence of an extensive or very active poetry-life, combined in any case with a natural taste for simple and touching lyrics, puts his enthralment with Thompson into strange prominence. In Thompson's most difficult poems he was even unaware of the obscurity. They were, as he read them aloud, his adopted speech. He was a good reader and his devotion communicated itself. The reading was the more welcome for the whole-hearted and affectionate manner of his bestowal of it on even passing acquaintances, as many old letters show, such as Mrs. Oscar Wilde's in 1894. "Come and read *Poems* to me. I want to become saturated with Francis Thompson; I am becoming so now, and he takes me up into regions of mysticism where I live a new life, and am happy!" And again: "Oscar was quite charmed with the lines that you read him of Francis Thompson." To Meynell's family the poems are still haunted by the sound of his voice, most of all any simpler lines where echo most easily lingers.

> By this, O Singer, know we if thou see.
> When men shall say to thee: Lo! Christ is here,
> When men shall say to thee: Lo! Christ is there,
> Believe them: yea, and this:—then art thou seer,
> When all thy crying clear
> Is but: Lo here! lo there!—ah me, lo everywhere!

IX

IN the course of years Meynell had built up a considerable journalistic connection—with all about him the noisy children whose support he was trying to earn. Sometimes the strain of word-spinning necessitated a couple of days' break, and a Quaker-like letter to his family would be squeezed in, like one in the year 1894.

Marine Parade, Brighton.

Darlings of my heart,

Your letters were all the more a delight to me this morning because I hardly expected them. I do hope that thou, my sweet wife, art feeling better, and not being fatigued today before thy dinner. I hope also that the darling daughter's cough is subsiding. The day here is sunny and cold. I saw Fr. Fawkes this morning for a few minutes. He has a very pleasant room in a very pleasant house—with Hegel's works much to the fore upon his shelves.

My host and hostess are only in lodgings here. The thing that passes for the Sea is at their door. But it is not the mighty Being: the spirit of the mighty Being will not stand a Parade, and the body of the Sea without the spirit is a disappointing affair.

I envy Everard the Latin lessons with his mother. I should know Latin now indeed if I had had such a dear instructress when I was a boy, tell him.

Expect me tomorrow when you see me. Very probably I shall be home to lunch. I know that my darling Monica will do the prudent thing about going to school with her cough. She knows I could not bear her to be ill and to suffer.

I love you all so much, my darling wife and children. And even the servants who wait on you have my gratitude. Believe me, with my devotion to all,

Your W.

Round about 1900 he had become literary adviser to the publishing firm of Burns and Oates, and constant attendance at their premises in Orchard Street was a new tie.

He was by now a figure in Catholic life, and whatever brand of man he was—or religion he had—must through many channels have been making its own impression. As a Catholic he had never quite shed his Quakerism. He had a Quaker flair for business and a Quaker's industry; was for lost causes, lame dogs and forlorn friends, and for individual interpretation of dogmas, and generous adjustments of errancies in others. He brought with him into Catholicism his Quaker experience of a strong sense of the reality and presence of God. He liked to quote what Disraeli said of himself—that in becoming a Christian he was "a completed Jew." Meynell might similarly have called himself "a completed Quaker." The Church that he joined was for him the Church of the Scriptures, and he was apt to see all problems in scriptural terms: mysteries of religion did not arise, effaced by: "I have yet many things to say to you, but you cannot bear them now." Another predominant text in his life was: "Inasmuch as ye did it to the least of my little ones ye did it unto me"; the line drawn between his neighbour and Christ was a fine one. So also was that between Nature and the Creator; he was always marvelling afresh at the sun, trees, water with its reflections—they were miracles performed before his eyes.

Thus even within the confines of his anonymous Catholic journalism, and of the practical considerations encumbent on the Burns and Oates business man he became, and between the lines of those countless office letters which soon streamed out from Burns and Oates (with just an extra touch of courtesy which, to one sometimes listening, seemed slightly in excess of what the short-hand pen taking them down could quite approve) there was a personality making itself known, something identifiable and recognizable.

From the earliest days of their journalism that personality, and that of his wife, had drawn in even the somewhat unlikely literary acquaintance. There are three letters from George Moore; the first of them is written soon after the publication of his *Flowers of Passion* in 1877.

61 Rue Condorcet. Tuesday

My dear Mrs. Meynell,

Have you seen the Journals they are simply terrific I do not really know how to act. The *World* was terribly scurrilous would you advise me to deign an answer. I would call out Yates if I were sure he would come out if he refused I would be absurd

I though[t] of going over to London to horsewhip him but am afraid of damages if it were only an affair of forty or fifty francs I would do it at once. I am really embarrased how to act It is dreadful to have left in that short line in "Bernice"

I should like to subscribe verses for some journal if I though[t] they would accept them

I send you an experiment if you think it good enough I will send it to the *Spectator* or to any other you might suggest.

The Exhibition opens on the first of May. Things are in a bad way here I am afraid that if it goes on much longer that we shall have another turn at the barricades.

Yours sincerely,

George Moore

PS Did you see *The Tatler* there is a very long article a column and a half not too bad if it comes in your way look at it December the 1st the last number If not too much trouble let me know if the verse I send you are good enough *I can't get the last line right* The kindest remembrances to Mr Meynell

61 Rue Condorcet

My dear Meynell,

A thousand apologies for not having answered your letter before.

I felt the justice of your advice to burn the verses on reading them. I sent them more as an échantillon (I cannot think of the English word) of a new form or what I believe to be one.

I am going to write a drama with a frenchman; he gives me the plan. I have also written some fifty or sixty pages of a new volume of poems to be called "rose of midnight" And you, you will tell me what you have been doing when you have time. Are you coming over in May? I am always at your dis position, if I can get your rooms or I can help you in any way I shall be delighted remember me in the kindest way to Mrs Meynell

A young lady has been pestering me with letters to write for some journal (I could not read the name she writes so badly) I sent her at last a little ballad, after the french manner, which I think good I will send you the paper when it appears.

I have been terribly abused for flowers of Passion, very well, but it succeeded Provost sold one week sixty-five copies and the book got a little known It would not have been so bad only for that detestable poem "Anna" What misfortune I had to publish it however it can't be helped now

Yours sincerely,

George Moore

Moore Hall Ballyglass Co Mayo

My dear Meynell,

Will you post the enclosed [a letter addressed to *The Times*] one is afraid to post them there the country is in an awful state.

Don't mention that I asked you to do this Things go back and a life is worth from the sum of five to twenty shillings I know lots of men who would do a job for me at the price regards to Mrs Meynell

Yours truly,

George Moore

Also among the many men and women in the writing world drawn into contact with Meynell's friendly and enterprising characteristics was the eccentric genius, Frederick William Rolfe—self-named Baron Corvo. Though not accepted as a candidate for the priesthood Corvo never wavered in his belief in his vocation; and in later years, in using his own name of Frederick Rolfe instead of the spurious Barony, he gave a deceptive twist to his signature by writing Fr. for Frederick, so that it might be read

WILFRID MEYNELL

in middle age

reason to dread the worst.

God bless and thank you
and yours, dear Wilfrid, for your
long and heroic kindness to me.

And remember if ever you
want to communicate with me,
the Poste Restante Charing Cross
will find me. I shall make a
point of going there every now
and then, in case such an
occasion should arise.

Ever and in all fates yours,

Francis Thompson.

I wish I had thought to make
my will before I left. You ought
to have it. But now it cannot
be done.

PART OF A LETTER from Francis Thompson
to Wilfrid Meynell—quoted on p. 165

"Father Rolfe." Meynell received from him a number of letters from Aberdeen, all with the same proud but urgent demand for help. This was in 1893, eleven years before the publication of *Hadrian the Seventh*; it was also before his letter-writing had acquired the furiously vindictive style which came later.

162 Shene St. Aberdeen. Feb. 21, 1893

My dear Sir,

Many thanks for your kind letter and enclosure. The latter I shall immediately lay out in the printing & publishing of some of my photographic studies & in the endeavour to get my work known.

One would certainly think that with my talents there would be no difficulty in getting employment but the misery I have endured during the last 7 years has only proved to me the impossibility of doing anything without either capital or a backer-up.

I know one thing I can safely say. It is that I have done more than any body would deem possible in the search for a sphere of work. I have answered close upon 500 advertizements & made myself a nuisance to every body by my pertinacity in worrying for interest. All for no good. I am a very methodical person & have kept a careful note & record of my every action.

As a matter of fact I know perfectly well that my powers & the singleness & rectitude of my conduct added to the simplicity of my habits & my divers interesting experiences of men & things, cannot possibly fail to meet with success when they have once found a sphere of operation & a chance.

Perhaps then you will let me point out two ways in which you can help me simply by wielding the influence you possess on my behalf.

I. You can take me on to your staff at Burns & Oates. There are 100 ways in which the originality & versatility of my mind could well be exercised there. I know that I should put out blossom to an astonishing extent in such an atmosphere & on the salary you should pay me I should be able to live & by degrees pay off my debts, for that is what worries me to death.

II. You can give me the use of some columns in your paper to plead my own cause. I have in MS a series of letters intended for a public character, illustrating my wants & the exact & easy thing it would be to correct them. Let me have the use of your columns to explain myself for a few weeks & I have a faith to move mountains. The condition of converts ought to be interesting to Catholics, ought it not?

One reason by the way why I fail to get work is my horrible appearance. A shabby badly-dressed person with a wan face haggard with the worry of 7 years torment & insufficient food stands no chance in this world.

Faithfully yours,
Frederick William Rolfe

Meynell introduced Rolfe to the owner of the *Aberdeen Free Press*, and he was offered a post as "reader," which however was not to his mind. A further effort must have been made ten years later when Meynell received this letter from Richard Whiteing, author of *No. 5 John Street*, enclosing letters from Corvo.

Vine Cottage, Northaw, Herts.
Oct. 5, 1903.

My dear Meynell,

. . . Would you mind looking over the enclosed and then sending them back to me. Read them in their sequence of date, the white before the blue. It is a curious case. I asked him to dinner at the Whitefriars Club on Friday and found a little weasel of a man almost tonsured with a close crop, and that indelible look of priest in every line of him which your seminaries seem to give whether they call or reject and which even Renan bore to the last day of his life. He tells a strange story of an attempt to live by learnedly popular books, and much resultant short commons as might be expected. I gave him a little lecture on not writing over peoples heads and he took it with a smile that might have meant anything though it was meekness and acquiescence as far as it met my eye. I also which was more to the purpose introduced him to a friend who promised to hand him on to people who might have a job in reviewing. I am going to try to find time for lessons in Italian from him.

Now can you do anything. You see he is one of yours in a double sense of faith and craftsmanship. *Try* just for my sake.

With kindest regards to Mrs. Meynell and love to the children.

Sincerely yours,
Richard Whiteing

It was rarely Meynell had a respite from close application to work, for as fast as he earned more for his children they grew to need more for their schooling, illnesses, holidays, etc. He formed the habit of totalling up his budget, with varying degrees of anxiety and relief, at the end of each week; and when Alice Meynell visited America in 1902 these records were sent to her for her own home-pining anxiety and relief.

This has been a good week:

Illustrated London News	£5	0	0
Burns & Oates	6	0	0
Daily Chronicle	6	0	0
Tatler	1	15	0
Tablet	2	0	0
Athenaeum	0	15	0
	21	10	0

—the best for several weeks.

I hope you think this a good record:

½ column *Pall Mall Gazette*	£1	10	0
2 columns *Illustrated London News*	4	0	0
13 *Daily Chronicle* paragraphs	3	5	0
3 columns *Athenaeum*	3	0	0
2¼ columns *Academy*	1	5	0
Burns & Oates	6	0	0
Tablet, 1 page	2	0	0
	21	0	0

It does not seem much perhaps but I can answer for its having taken a good deal of making, and I feel very happy to be able to make for 2 weeks running, without your aid, the necessary £20. If I can keep that up till your ever and daily desired return I shall feel I have deserved a holiday, which I hope I shall be able to think is better than having one.

Last week was so wretched a one I did not dare to pan it out on paper. This is not much better:

Daily Chronicle	£3	10	0
Pall Mall Gazette	0	10	0
Tablet	2	0	0
Burns & Oates	6	0	0
	12	0	0

I seem to be working very hard, seventeen hours one day this week—which has given me a blear eye—& yet not to be making a fortune.

Alice Meynell, persuaded to lecture while she was in the United States, and sending back the £20 of her fee, made one week's combined budget up to £40. "That is something like a week," Meynell wrote, "thanks Dearest to you." He had the characteristic of being particularly open-handed. "Do not think you need worry about money," he wrote to her. "It is not so. I think you should spend a lot in tips, etc. Do not economise." When the growing-up family asked him for money for their increasing social activities and their games-struck or dress-struck needs, he had a way of delving into his pocket and holding out the money flat on his hand, without looking at it, for them to help themselves —with a reassuring air of oblivion towards the incident. To one of the daughters visiting Italy with her mother he wrote: "You will make a splendid comrade, and a darling one, for your mother. I do not want you to be stingy in any way. You must spend as much not as little as you can, for when there are only two of you, you cannot cost any more than we can easily afford."

What a family afforded then reads almost voluptuously now. At Palace Court, cook, house-parlourmaid and nurse were a modest staff. The daughters as they in turn left school at the age of sixteen would take on the housekeeping to relieve her whom

George Meredith called "their pencilling Mamma." Letters written by the young family to their mother when she was in America cover the domestic side of life pretty thoroughly, and show how a portion of the funds was disposed. When a birthday occurs the reigning housekeeper writes: "It is nearly time to dress for dinner. We have got: first, soup; then an entrée of kidneys with mushrooms; and as a joint roast turkey with French beans and potatoes, followed by Chestnut pudding, and black-berry tart and cream. Then pineapple, which I got for 2/- because it has a rather shabby appearance, melon, bananas, walnuts, chestnuts and sweets. I call that an excellent filling meal." Another daughter, equally absorbed in menus, wrote: "I today resigned my post of housekeeper. I ordered a large joint of beef for lunch, and two very large chickens for dinner tonight. But tomorrow and the day after being days of abstinence, Monica had to go down and countermand my orders. How could I show my face as housekeeper after that?" The letters were full and frequent, abounding in the incidents of family life. "Francis Thompson came very late to dinner, so he had his up in the library where we were. In the middle of his dinner he went and stood near Father to read him a poem, and the innocent cat jumped up in his chair and finished all his good dinner for him." The years 1901-2 were the time when the game then called "ping-pong" was introduced—at any rate to Palace Court, and was played furiously. Most unlikely visitors came under the spell. One match, pure opera bouffe, played to derisive yells, was reported "between Brin[1] and Francis Thompson." "Brin" was stout and good-natured and unwieldy; the players were well matched, for neither could contact the ball, and Francis Thompson's pipe fell from his mouth in the energetic action of missing it.

Practical jokes, once conceived by Meynell, were never skimped. A solicitor friend, a co-religionist, was disappointed of being selected by the Duke of Norfolk as a steward on the occasion of the Duke's leading a great Catholic pilgrimage to

[1] Bernard Whelan; best man at the Meynells' wedding, and author of *An Architect in Exile*.

Rome. The stewards were to supervise the send-off from Victoria, and were to be distinguished by a rosette on their coat-lapel. Meynell's friend had quite fancied that the Duke might appoint him. After listening to his thinly-veiled dissatisfaction on the eve of the pilgrimage, Meynell and his son Everard spent the evening fixing many-coloured ribbons on to a piece of cardboard the size of a saucer, and posting it to their friend as from the Duke; and they had the gratification next day of seeing him the most conspicuous figure on the platform. As the stewards had been asked to yield up their rosettes on the train, the last sight Meynell had of his friend, as it moved off, showed him battling his way to the Duke for that purpose.

Alice Meynell wrote to one of the family away from home: "I am glad to say that a plot to make a teazle crawl in Brin's bed last night came to nothing. It was to be moved by a string that passed under the door. Your father and Everard devoted much time to the preparation, but it did not work."

With his turn for practical resourcefulness he must have been at home with the ingenious firm of Field and Tuer of the Leadenhalle Presse, for whom in the eighteen-eighties he had acted for some time as reader and editor. This publishing house showed a dexterity and invention which must have shocked the established Trade. As side-lines, it published the first writing-pads of thin ruled paper, in habitual use by both Wilfrid and Alice Meynell (so that "fetch me a Tuer pad" was the commonest of commands to the children); it invented and sold a paste, "Stickphast," on the labels of which its name still survives; it provided materials for home ink-making. An important contribution to bookmaking was the opportunity Field and Tuer offered to Joseph Crawhall (like Meynell, a Newcastle man), who made hundreds of cuts in the chap-book fashion, which were hand-coloured. It was they who in 1880 published *Journals and Journalism, with a Guide for Literary Beginners*, by John Oldcastle [W. M.], cased in half pigskin, price 3s. 6d. They certainly announced (but evidence of publication cannot be found) a sixteen-penny series of classics to be edited by Meynell.

Meynell's vast amount of writing was done at the library table, where his pad would rest on a depth of other papers; one leg was curled under him, for he was not apt to take conventional positions; and when work was over he fancied sitting on the rug by the fire. Indeed when he was once asked to take the chair at some meeting at the Kensington Town Hall, in refusing he pleaded that even in his own home he too often found he had abandoned his chair for the floor, an unfortunate tendency in a chairman.

He wrote facilely; syntax, grammar, spelling were as if inborn. It was a rare grammatical doubt which made him apply to his club acquaintance Oscar Wilde for a verdict. Meynell notes: "There was a correspondence in the *Athenaeum* as to the grammar of Cardinal Newman's sentence: 'To Wesley you must go, and such as him.' Matt. Arnold supported this accusative which I had criticized, and I appealed to Oscar to express an opinion."

Bamff, Alyth, Perthshire.
[August, 1890.]

My dear Meynell,

I am far away from the *Athenaeum* in the midst of purple heather and silver mist—such a relief to me, Celt as I am, from the wearisome green of England—I only like green in art—this is one of my many heresies.

When I am back in a few days I must look up the point at issue. In what a fine "temper" Newman always wrote! the temper of the scholar. But how subtle was his simple mind!

Pray give my kind regards to your wife.

Believe me truly yours,
Oscar Wilde

Meynell's journalism, past, present, and to come—given that he had a just and generous outlook—was made mostly of combined facility and emergency industry. He did not feel the lack of foreign languages nor of studious knowledge of literature. In late life, with cheerful arrogance, he belittled academic training and teased scholars and scholarship: "Dull dogs trying to decide whether the battle of Marathon was fought on a Thursday or a Friday." He spoke as one who had mostly got through on decency, versatility, and the turn of a phrase.

His free-lance journalism was of a far wider kind through the eighties and nineties and at the turn of the century than a writer would have the opportunity—and perhaps the versatility —for to-day. As weekly journalism was nearly always anonymous, editors did not then, as they might to-day, feel it necessary to tie a writer to their paper. Thus he reviewed week in week out for the *Athenaeum* and the *Academy*; paragraphed daily for the *Daily Chronicle*; wrote articles almost monthly for the *Art Journal*; gossiped and commented every week in *The Tablet*, and occasionally in the *Illustrated London News*, though, as a reviewer at large, knowing little or nothing of his subject-matter that was not presented in the book reviewed.

Free-lance journalism was by no means lacking in editorial discipline. On March 10, 1899, Charles Lewis Hind, editor of the *Academy* writes:

My dear Wilfrid,

The pressure upon our space is so tremendous that I want to ask you to confine Memoirs to one page (£1 10. 0). It's an excellent feature and very welcome, but I think you should keep the idea of Memoirs well before you—that is longish, well-reasoned pars. hanging upon some personality or event of the week. We are not anxious to have pars. like the Zangwill, or the John Lane, or the Duchess of Sutherland, as such matters come under the heading of our Literary Week. I think the idea of the page is something that might conceivably be useful to future historians of manners, and of men and women who (not always in the public eye) are making the history of the day. Hope to see you Sunday aft. Of course when you get such a plum as the price Morley got for the Gladstone, a short par. serves the case well. The first col. of Memoirs this week is excellent—just the thing. But *do* be prompter with copy. This week was a record.

Yours,
L. Hind

Writing as near as he could to this specification Meynell received from the *Academy* £10 10s. 0d. as the highest of his monthly cheques (for weekly work), and £6 as the least—figures which themselves point to his need of many such assignments in journalism to supply himself with an income.

When, in the 1920's, Meynell could write pretty well where he pleased and what he pleased, he chose as his mouthpieces the *Dublin Review*, the quarterly which he had published at Burns and Oates and invested with a typographical format better in its kind than anything since or immediately before, and the *Review of Reviews*, into the editorship of which he had helped Daniel O'Connor.[1] He was writing now not against time and for necessary money but to help magazines in which he was interested by a sprightly and readable exposition of views and enthusiasms. These multitudinous pieces are ephemeral, but are mirrors of his mind. He chides Sir Henry Lucy because in his *Diary* he says of the suffragists that their "performances" should be "put down with a stronger hand than by the action of the magistrates." Meynell says: "He should read Rebecca West to get into a saner frame of mind. In *The Judge* we find a retrospect that must revive in all men of chivalry their homage to the women who worked in ways the most repulsive to themselves for the emancipation of their sex." Reviewing Norman Angell's *Is Britain to Live?* he says: "We may not annex our neighbour's land because we believe we can put it to better use than he; but we have taken vast territories under this plea. Heard-of and unheard-of cruelties and evictions and death have been inflicted on native races because a white asserted his superiority over a red, a yellow, a brown, or a black. Under our colour, as well as our colours, we fought our battles, bloody for our unaccoutred foes, almost harmless to ourselves."

The *Diaries* of Sir Algernon West give him an easy chance to air his distaste for politics and politicians (but Disraeli would always have been excepted): "There is a letter from Gladstone in

---

[1] A man of many literary projects not always practical, whom W. M. had helped to establish as a publisher soon after the end of the First World War by finding him a partner, Herbert Wilson. The firm, under the style of Herbert and Daniel, contributed to the typographic revival of that decade, but was short-lived.

which he advises his secretary to go away for a holiday, adding, however, of London, 'But the place is a great tonic.' That is just what was behind Disraeli's remark that the best air in Europe blew at the top of St. James's St., and it is the only saying of Gladstone's in all the book that is at all refreshing." Reviewing a book on George Meredith, Meynell writes:

> The reader who is no idle one wishes to find in his author not only companionship for all that is best in himself, but for something that is better and higher than he himself has reached. Readers during the last half of the past century who wanted to be in the company of an intellectual superior fulfilled their need when they took their Meredith volumes to their heads and their hearts. We hear much of his obscurities. But you might nearly as well quarrel with a grape because of its indigestible pips, or buy your grocer's shelled walnuts in order to save the preliminary exercise with the crackers which is necessary to their full enjoyment.

And there is Meynell's characteristic family feeling—backward to parents and forward to children and their children, in a contribution to the *Dublin Review* in 1925:

> . . . Is there not one neglected plea to be advanced in extenuation of Byron's often only-braggart surface infidelities? Sir Walter Scott predicted of him that, had he lived, he would have become a Catholic and even the postulant of a strict religious order. Remembering that, it is even a little startling to note that all Byron's descendants (like Sir Walter's own) are actually votaries of that Church, obedient to its discipline. Heredity is a strange, writhing, and elusive serpent: none can really capture and diagnose it. But if we are to say of Byron, as is commonly done, that this defect he had from his father and that from his mother, may we not even more plausibly bring his descendants as well as his progenitors into the reckoning? A man lives in his descendants even more than in his ancestors. The family tree must be rated by its new branches no less than by its old; there is no finality. . . .

Reviewing the *Life* of Alfred Lyttelton by his second wife, Meynell cannot pass without comment her phrase: "he was deeply and simply religious but possessed often by a mercurial roguish spirit of fun." "Instead of 'but,' " he writes, "we should have written 'and'—there is really no antithesis between piety and pranks."

Examples could be multiplied, but these will suffice, of the fact that Meynell in reviewing books was constantly reviewing and revealing himself.

That he could be a controversialist on the side of authority, even at the expense of out-arguing someone dear to him, is shown by a leading article he wrote for *The Tablet* in 1899. Dr. Mivart—an old and close friend, it will be remembered—had inveighed in *The Times* against the Pope's silence in the Dreyfus affair. Meynell wrote:

"Out of strength came sweetness." Not less perplexing than the old riddle is the new one of this week, when out of the Dreyfus case comes incongruously a plea for more Papal intervention in mundane affairs. The mouth of the dead lion as the store-house of honey offered no surprises of locality equal to those presented on Tuesday by the columns of *The Times*. The most powerful paper in that realm of England which boasts that the Pope has no jurisdiction within it, now sends forth to the city and the world of Protestantism the amazing message that Leo XIII has been guilty in the Dreyfus affair, not of speech, but of silence—a silence that is "deplorable" . . . We are set at once to wondering when and what Leo XIII was to speak, and on this point it is the silence of Dr. Mivart that we deplore. . . . The presumption of the clamourers for speech must clearly be that the Pope, after the Rennes verdict, should have denounced it—a presumption indeed. Well, if the Pope had, his speech would have been found "intolerable" by *The Times*, as certainly as by the French clergy; by Dr. Mivart himself, we venture to assert, as by the French army. For these are among the consequences. No Pope can do more than trust to his representatives and pro-consuls in the far provinces of the Church for reports of its daily doings, for despatches from its field of warfare against the forces that are hostile to righteousness. We do not need to ask Dr. Mivart what should be the report of the French Bishops about the Anti-Semite movement; for he tells us—in opposition to Mr. Bodley, an eyewitness on the spot—that the French clergy and episcopate, as a body, are involved in the race hatred of the Jew! Leo XIII could but have taken his reports of the Dreyfus case from these witnesses—these untrustworthy witnesses in Mr. Mivart's view—and, misled himself, have formulated the falsehood with the chance of a confusion of right and wrong resulting from the speaker's lofty mission. . . . Mr. Dick, in *David Copperfield*, could not draw up a statement of his own woes without introducing an allusion to the King's head. With Dr. Mivart, the omnipresent figure is Galileo; that great name adorns all his pages; but the moral of the history of Galileo—at any rate of *his* story of Galileo—is nothing if not this—that ecclesiastics, perhaps with the best of intentions, have transgressed their province not too little, but too much. Nay, we gather from Dr. Mivart that in our own day—in his own day—the Roman Congregations have been too willing to press in where angels even—"birds of happiness" though they be—might fear to fly. Yet it is this minimizer on one page who, on the next, cries out with the daughters of the horse-leech, "More, more."

A last glance at Wilfrid Meynell's journalism is somehow typical of life and letters then. In a so-much-smaller London than that of to-day, literary people were much known to each other, and the authors dealt with by reviewers were often their friends. Reviews being anonymous, a little log-rolling which need not falsify resulted, and Meynell could for example write in more than one paper about the fine autobiography of his brother-in-law Sir William Butler. Authors' requests for reviews, which then beset reviewers, were a corollary of this situation; and Mrs. Hamilton King, whose abbreviated friendship with Francis Thompson is described in Chapter VII, provides almost a comedy among such episodes. When her *Letters and Recollections of Mazzini* were about to be published in 1912 she wrote to her friend Wilfrid Meynell a précis of the points she wished him to stress in a review she hoped he would write in *The Tablet*—particularly the fact that her publishing now the documents of her enthusiasm for Mazzini involved no possibility of offence against her Catholic orthodoxy. A second letter from her explains that she thought Meynell was proprietor or editor of *The Tablet*, but still begs for his services there. A third seeks to clinch the matter, but with a light touch encloses a draft for his review, to begin: "This book is harmless but silly."

The girlish letters contained in it were not thought silly by Mazzini, whose replies are gentle, comprehending, humble. Here are three passages from what the British girl wrote to her unknown Italian hero:

Chardstock, August 16, 1862.

Mazzini!

Forgive me for intruding on one whose every moment is precious, but I can keep silence no longer: and needing counsel and advice I come, to seek it from him who has long been the guiding star of my aspirations, and whom, though so great and to me unknown, I approach with the confidence of an old familiar friend, and the mild father of my spiritual life. . . .

Mazzini, who for his crown of laurel wears the crown of thorns, has been ever to me too sacred and exalted a mystery for my song to reach. When I come into his presence I find no words, but only tears and burning of the heart. Obedience is the best homage to render him. . . .

They blame Mazzini for sending so many to death. Those died happy; for myself I would ask no better fate. This I ask: is the final hour of action come? or must I wait for a future? I would not miss it when it comes: only, remember this,—you have in me one ever ready to obey you, and to serve your holy cause, to leave all and follow you at your summons on whatever mission you appoint. Test my fidelity as you will: only, I pray you, of your generosity, not to impose upon me anything repugnant to my conscience, nor that would cut me off from my present sphere of life without insuring to me a new one.

I send you my own likeness that you may know the face of one of your most faithful disciples.

This letter is for your eyes alone. Farewell, great spirit,

whom God knows now, whom men will know hereafter. I kiss your hands. Accept me and command me as yours.

Harriet Eleanor Baillie Hamilton

These letters, with Mazzini's quiet replies, might, says Meynell in the review of which Mrs. Hamilton King was not disappointed,

have been the correspondence between a confessor of renown and a devoted girl, avid to sacrifice herself to her religious vocation. . . . As a matter of fact Miss Hamilton did not go into the field—she did not become the "Theodora" of *Lothair*. . . . Perhaps no movement in all the world's history has evoked so generous an enthusiasm as that accorded by men like Meredith and women like Mrs. Browning to the Unity-of-Italy-movement in the last century. All gross things went by the board—the idea of liberty filled the vision of idealists, who had no crystal of the future in which to discern the breach of all they most loved, the bond of human brotherhood. Mazzini lived long enough to disown Garibaldi and to refuse to look out of the window of the carriage in which he traversed a Rome obsessed, as he thought, by a monarchy. But his was a light disappointment compared with that which has awaited many an English lover of Italy in the modern developments of her story, her vanity that preys on the vitals of her own poor, the big navy that needs a big salt-tax, the acknowledgement of religion only that it may be flouted; the putrid literature, the vulgar art, and, finally, that unprovoked attack in Tripoli, which leaves us cold to the futilities of a Bomba.

Mrs. Hamilton King knitted for bazaars in aid of the "Venice and Rome Emancipation Fund," and her husband sent Mazzini several cheques for £5. We know the price of living has gone up, but might not have remembered the price of revolutions! Mazzini wrote to Mrs. King on April 1, 1867, that he had no hope of conducting a successful invasion of Rome since that would cost £8,000.

The *Weekly Register* was not thriving; its rival, *The Tablet*, held the field, there being hardly room for two weekly papers more similarly sectarian than they were dissimilarly political.

Meynell sold it in 1899 to a Mr. Boland for £840. It was a relief to be spared the drudgery of its editorship, but into the hole in industry then created he poured new enterprise, the bulkiest part of which was two heavy volumes on Disraeli, which however were light entertainment. Ever since his first reading of *Sybil*, Meynell's devotion to the man who had so much zeal for a young England to improve workers' conditions amounted to hero-worship; and he had amassed a hoard of his sayings and doings to be formed in 1903 into *An Unconventional Biography*. This Dizzy-worship, which turned him then Tory in support of social legislation to deal with existing evils, cutting across his other loyalty to the Home Rule sympathies of Liberalism, had made him in love with even the merely anecdotal aspect of his hero, and the book is a book of anecdotes based on Disraeli's own sayings.

> To be a biographer proper [Meynell wrote in his Preface] would indeed be beyond my capacities; and in apology I should like to say that the book came rather fortuitously into being. Disraeli's novels had opened for me as a schoolboy the windows on life. More than all, he made me thus early conscious of "The Two Nations," the Rich and the Poor, who must yet be one. I had been a butt of my school-fellows, and enjoyed so being, for learning and reciting the perorations of my hero's current speeches. In one of my holidays, I had enjoyed the adventure of following him from the House to Downing Street—it is the only way that some of us can follow in the footsteps of the great. As I grew older, he gave the personal interest to politics which made that "dull trade," as Stevenson dubs it, almost a romance of reality. Everyone I met who had known him I eagerly "pumped," and for my own purposes I started a Disraeli scrap-book by which I educated myself on the various disputed episodes of his life.

By way of dedication, "having this bunch of Primroses to give," he offered the book to Wilfrid Blunt, adding:

> There are auguries that favour the conjunction of his name and yours. You, like him, have loved the Arab, man and horse;

and it is my faith that had you lived of old in Egypt, you, vexing the souls of Pharaohs, would have solaced and shortened the captivity of the Children of Israel—Disraeli's own fathers. "Egypt for the Egyptians" on your lips had then meant "Let this people go!" And I recall the time when, even in our Island, you, an accepted poet, pursued the fickle jade Politics, enduring sorrow for her sake. Disraeli, on the other hand, paramount in Parliament, was hooted from Parnassus. The pleasure of an antithesis tempts me to make allusion to this one failure of his in a career that otherwise reconciles, over the range of romance and to the very verge of miracle, faith with fulfilment, purpose with achievement, wish with accomplishment, dream with daily reality.

But Blunt on receiving the book wrote:

You must not, however, call me a Dizzy-*worshipper*, as you do in your dedication. I am a hundred miles away from that. Aesthetically our good Jew was a terrible Philistine; and politically (I say it with some timidity to you his apologist) a very complete *farceur*. I don't like to call him anything worse than that. "Mountebank" and *charlatan* are abusive terms which imply deception for an ignoble end, and of this there is no sign, for his ambition was pure of all money calculations. Only you cannot persuade me that he ever for an instant took himself seriously as a *British* statesman, or expected any but the stolid among his contemporaries to accept him so.

This "unconventional biography" was an excursion—Meynell's only one—into full-sized book-making. His own version of it was that he wrote it so much to please himself that he must not grumble if it did not suit others. But it was successful, in a moderate way. It was something he had to do. His brother Samuel wrote from Newcastle: "Dearest Brother, You have fulfilled the vows of your youth." In 1927 he recast the book into a single volume. A point to be cleared up in relation to this new issue was which of two men first proposed Queen Victoria's health as the new "Empress of India" at a dinner at Windsor Castle. Through their common friend, Lady Leslie, the Duke of Connaught sent Meynell his underlined impression:

As far as I can remember (it is now many years ago) *I* gave the Queen's health as "Empress of India" at the dinner at Windsor Castle, on the night of the day of the proclamation of her new title at a great Durbar at Delhi held by Lord Lytton (Viceroy of India). Lord Beaconsfield & Lord George Hamilton were, I remember, present at that dinner. My mother in her letters *distinctly* mentions the fact of *my* having proposed *her health*—and I am sure that it *must have been so*—as she was *always most accurate* in her statements, which were invariably written down the evening of the day on which any particular event occurred—which she considered worthy of notice— Although *not certain*—I am *quite convinced* in my own mind that *I* and not Lord Beaconsfield proposed her health on the occasion referred to.

Small books that Meynell wrote were mostly suitable for Catholic readers. *The Cousins*, in 1895, was fiction in form, not much longer than a short story in length, and turned on the segregated conservatism of a group of old Catholic families, and the greater enlightenment of one of its young members. "You describe a phase of Catholic life in England utterly unknown to me," his friend, Sir Francis Burnand, the Catholic editor of *Punch*, wrote to him. "It exists & therefore as it ought not to exist you do well to satirise it—that is, if the satire can kill. It is Effeminate Romanism in contradistinction to Robust Catholicism. It is Oscar Wildeism in religion—& I see my coined word has 'deism' in it." Into this and his other anonymous brochures the author trots every predilection he has (generally including Thompson); he is apt also to offer an individual whimsy as proof-proper to the argument in hand, for so much do his writings engross his own affiliations, down to extraneous detail, that they are like so many family albums of his own mind.

In 1902, for instance, *Faith Found in London* was a fervent and spirited tract, *Being a Relation of the Strange Adventures of Count Marco Caradori Who came hither for the Coronation of Edward VII and Who in our Babylon discovered His Own Spiritual Crown.* Not only are Catholic churches and charities visited, but by anecdote, reference, coincidence, and argument Catholicism is wrenched— for the benefit of the astonished Count who had come prepared for an agreeable spell of paganism—from the stones of London as if they were those of a Holy City. It is special pleading (scoring a success however with the Count!)—eloquent, discursive, emotional, factual, fanciful. In it he draws on his mind's current account for the stock comments he had to make on affairs, and the narrative makes where necessary a détour to include them. On one page he airs a permanent irritation against something worse than mere journalism as it occurred in the Boer War newspaper reports:

> We fall back, they fly; they run away, we retire; we have a mishap, they a defeat; we withdraw where they are driven back; and we have a reverse when they are wiped out and utterly routed; their preparations are cunningly calculated, and ours are prudent prevision; our soldiers are plucky where theirs were foolhardy; our staying power was their stubbornness; we were daring, they reckless; they murdered our spies, and we most righteously punished theirs; oh the babiness of it all!

Quotations from Francis Thompson and Alice Meynell crop up anonymously in the text as if they were everybody's common speech of every day—as they do in much of his writing, where Manning and Disraeli lag not far behind. (Blunt wrote to him once that he presumed he was back in London, since Disraeli was once more cropping up in the *Daily Chronicle* paragraphs.)

In 1908, *The Story of the [Eucharistic] Congress* was likewise *A Record of Things seen and heard in Catholic London*.

Then in 1916 a strange thing happened. Not a religious but a lay tract, this time, was provoked by the war. The brand of philistinism now satirized, in the same faintly fictional discursiveness, was that of the comfortable rich woman aghast at having to yield her footman to the ranks; and again enlightenment reaches her and prevails. But on this occasion the subject and the method caught on with a large public, and soon a round 100,000 copies were sold, and with *Aunt Sarah and the War* Meynell had the unlooked-for experience of finding himself a popular, though anonymous, author. It was followed by *Who Goes There?* in the same genre, also successful.

In three small collections of verse—*Verses and Reverses, Rhymes with Reasons,* and *The New Young*—his word-dexterity is of a kind widely abounding nowadays in weekly competitions but more unfamiliar in his time. The *Athenaeum* defined his quality when it wrote: "The best things are so neatly turned that few living men could equal them. He has Hood's delightful effrontery of punning and Locker's lightness of tread, and he has a gift—peculiar to himself—of interweaving with his metrical waltzings serious expressions of deep feeling. He is an earnest wit." He played his word-games with himself all his life. "Anagrams may some day be a popular diversion," he accurately wrote; "it was a good enough pastime for Plato; for St. Bernard too, who hailed the new Eve with an Ave." Alice Meynell, doubtful about puns of any kind, is remembered questioning with extra incredulity: "Not puns on *names*, surely!" But whether of puns or anagrams, it was a gay career not to be checked. He turned the name of his friend Father Rice into Eric and wrote to him:

> "Little by little" not
> We loved you—lot by lot.

A verse refers to ". . . Charles Lamb (and may I without qualm Remark his anagram is Balm)"; St. Paul's is the Wren-nest; Noah exclaims, "Ah no!" One instance of word-play refers to a statement by Mendelssohn of his father's disapproval of his musical studies, and the state of constant irritation and argument between them, until it occurred to young Mendelssohn that he might speak a great deal of truth and yet avoid the particular truth obnoxious to his father.

> The happy Maestro Mendelssohn
> One harmony essayed,
> Of all his works the least that's known,
> Yet loveliest to be played!

His Songs, and Songs that have no words,
His Night Dream's Overture,
The gentle melody of the Lord's
Elijah,—these endure:

Men worship him for such:
But I—I, rather,
That he, with filial touch,
Composed—his Father!

Again:

Men "fall in love," and soar the skies
    From earth's profoundest prison:
O change the word as there it lies—
    Not *fallen* in love, but *risen*.

And here he reads an anagrammatic lesson in "A New Commandment."

Put up thy sword into its sheath!
I (Peter's foundling) hear, O Lord;
But all around
Louder is heard
The ominous sound
Of angry *words*,
Which turn, a letter moved, to *sword*,
And, with like easy shift, to wars
That Love abhors.

This New Commandment be the Lord's
Put up thy word into its breath,
O sheathe thy words!

In the daily incidents of friendship and companionship he was incalculable, and in trivial encounters the exigencies of a moment were turned in his own way. Taking back to a tailor a new suit for alteration, he teased him with the doubtful reassurance: "But I would rather go to a bad tailor who is a good man than a good tailor who is a bad man." His oldest age did not diminish the habit.

When he heard that a granddaughter had got a "first" at Oxford he wired to her: "*It must be a frost.*" He took another granddaughter aback, when she decided her ambition was to have an orphanage when she grew up, by pointing out that he was eligible for admittance. Writing to friends just made he would sign himself truthfully at the age of ninety: "Your oldest friend."

X

THOMPSON'S notebook habit was prodigious, in more ways than one—in the number of the notebooks, and in their description printed on the outside in stationers' fancy lettering: "The PRODIGIOUS Faint-Ruled Exercise Book. 100 pages. 1*d*." Multiplication tables were thrown in on the back cover. Into a vast number of these penny exercise books he wrote the whole literature of a man's mind; they are as clear on one page as indecipherable on another; the pencilling is faint or confident; the contents may start from either end; in some exigencies the unnumbered pages need turning backwards to follow the course of an entry. There is no facet of his life and thought not reflected in these books; he knew they were himself, and he preserved them as instinctively as one saves one's skin; they formed his only library, since he did not possess more than six other books in all. He was a thinker, not a talker: the notebooks were the outcome.

Even to him it must have been difficult to retrace his steps through the maze should he want to find anything; and many a "MEM" written to himself must have faded into its thumbed oblivion before it was ever acted on—even though it might be pitched on a high note of urgency with heavy underlinings, in his distrust of himself. "MEM. MOST PRESSING. Write to I— *instantly, or you are lost.*" And a day later: "Send the letter to I— as early as possible in morning." And a day later again: "Get shirt out of durance [pawn] first thing in morning: send the letter to I—." "MEM. Write, in first leisure time, notes on Hebrew-Punic alphabet."

In an early book, writing as an ex-seminarian, and in a monastic atmosphere, he makes an "Order of Day."

Brief prayer on Waking or Dressing
Early Mass (if possible)

Breakfast
Work
Dinner
Walk,—or if weather & health too bad
    Copying Work, or Letters.
Tea
Work; if too unwell
    Copying Work, Letters or Reading
Supper
Night Prayers. Examination of Conscience.

When this order regularly in practice, can consider supplementary times & modes of prayer. This elementary plan first.

But it was for rough drafts that the books had their chief use; and in notes for poems, essays, and reviews there are beginnings later developed or lost in their sheer numbers—such as an idea on the function of poetry being to "see & restore the Divine idea of things."

Job, Isaiah, Ezekiel, all ye prophets with ye amazing Apocalypse at their head, are but that Imagination (God's) stooping to ye tongue of ye nursery. Yet ye Apocalypse is so big with meanings that every sentence yields significances for endless study. And it is just ye child's apologue of that inconceivably enormous Mind, whose nature-book is ye Universe, & its compendium Man. He cannot read himself—that compendium is beyond him—he is too big for himself; so that he takes up, as an easier labour ye reading of God, & is seriously angry with his Author's obscurity. Yet, in one germ-idea of that mind a wilderness of Plato's would be more unnoticeably lost than flies inside St. Paul's. But, secondly, there is an added reason for human confusion, which is nearly always ignored. The world—the Universe—is a fallen world. When people try to understand the Divine plans, they forget that everything is not as it was designed to be. And with regard to any given thing you have first to discover, if you can, how far it is as it was meant to be. That should be precisely ye function of poetry—to see & restore ye divine idea of things, freed from ye disfiguring accidents of their Fall.

In his rough drafts the variant versions of words and phrases give the pages the appearance of diagrams. Here are two verses of "The Kingdom of God"—finished, and in process of formation.

Does the fish soar to find the ocean,
The eagle plunge to find the air—
That we ask of the stars in motion
If they have rumour of Thee there?

Not where the wheeling systems darken
And our benumbed conceiving soars!—
The drift of pinions, would we harken,
Beats at our own clay-shuttered doors.

Does ye fish
Who bids fish soar into the ocean

The eagle plunge to find ye air,

That we/men cry to the stars in motion

If they/men have/hear whisper of thee there?

Not where ye rolling/hurtling/whirling/rumbling systems darken

Wherto our numbed conjecture/conceiving soars

The draft/storm/drift of pinions, would we harken.

beats at our clay/earth -shuttered doors.

our earthy/clayey -shuttered doors

our shut/closed and earthy/clayey doors

156

Sometimes the alternative words rise in a neat column on the page; he was thinking on paper. In one note he must have been considering this kind of patient exploration, and also of the violence of expression with which he was charged when he wrote:

There are word-tasters and word-swillers. Unfortunately ye two are confounded. Because ye tasteless many among writers indulge in orgies of "strong" & "picturesque" language unrecking of fitness & delicate adjustment of meaning, a hue & cry goes out against ye few whom they ignorantly imitate, ye few whose love of language goes down to ye sensitive roots of words, ye few who never bang on a strong word like a tin kettle to deafen ye ears of ye groundlings, but use it because it is ye one word which is ye exact vehicle for a strong thing; because it is not *a* strong word but *ye* strong word culled carefully from many strong words. These are connoisseurs in words. The others are drunkards in words. Like ye dram drinker, they have swallowed language till their palate has lost all distinction but that of coarse stimulus. Is it intoxicant enough? Is it hot in the mouth? Whether it be ye best, ye right word, they care nought, so it blisters the tongue.

Though these notes are those of a man committing a teeming mind to the shabby sheet of paper always at hand, for this present purpose it is the rare personal note which stands out as the pages are turned. There is sometimes a domestic shopping-list, including: "TODAY: Spoon, Knife & Cup. TOMORROW [but many of these to-morrows never came]: Shirt, Hat, & perhaps Ink." Or suddenly there is a cry from the depth of experience and emotion —and this may perhaps relate to his friend of the streets, the girl "Ann":

Often since have I longed to encounter her; to thank her for that graciously delicate whisper which brought such healing to my hurt indignant heart. But I never shall, till ye Day which evens all debts. It is not like that these lines will ever have meeting with her sweet sad eyes. Could that be, I would desire she might read in them a gratitude which passes speech, & ye accumulated silences of many intervening years.

157

In another note he defines himself as poet. "After ye Return to Nature, ye Return to God. Wordsworth was ye poet of ye one. I would be ye poet of ye other." And of his poetry's fate:

For me to write or speak at all is to resign myself to ye knowledge that I am, in ye present, addressing very few. It would be almost impossible, because quite futile, for me to write were I not convinced that ye few will one day be ye many. Nothing has so impressed me in ye utterances of critics, even ye best disposed towards me, as ye profound incapacity of almost every man in these days to conceive that I mean, or *can* mean, ye thing I say. That I should, for instance, actually & in naked fact believe,—that I should have a pregnant & familiar sense of a world within ye world seen of eye & touched of hand, seems to them so patently untenable that they seek every explanation of my words, resort to any gloss, in the effort to escape their steadfast & direct assertion, to avoid an hypothesis so monstrous. They do not even dream of considering it.

"MEM. Revise Pastoral; & get buttons if any possible chance."

What are represented also are his jocose moods, but those are hardly the pages to linger on. He was not humourless, but it was schoolboy humour, towards which it is difficult for the adult not to be condescending. The bit of doggerel beginning below extends to twenty-nine stanzas before it runs itself out with "tout est finny."

> Now Doris Biggs was a pretty maid
>   Who dealt in the fish-line
> And so she hooked young William Higgs
>   Of the Pike and Gudgeon sign.
>
> But soon she loved another man
>   Who worked at the Red Earl,
> And was engaged again, for she
>   Was an engaging girl.
>
> Poor William sought her where she plied
>   A brisk fish-mongering trade
> Unheedful of his woes, because
>   She was a sell-fish maid.

"O Doris Biggs, how can you thus
    Pursue your finny sales?
The time has been, alas! you weighed
    Me in quite other scales. . . ."

Thompson, more than most, was two men; and this type of humour, on a par with that of the man who tells a "good story" —humour boxed for occasional use—but who misses the constant wit of life itself, belonged to the pedestrian man Thompson could be. He might not tell a good story, but he would please himself with the composition of an inferior limerick. Of the flash of un-invented wit implicit in the moments of living to the X-ray eye, he was oblivious. He could not perceive absurdity—but he could provide it, as when he was present at a family Shakespeare reading and after a customary exploration of his pockets inter-rupted Desdemona's death by exclaiming: "Here's a go, Mrs. Meynell, I have lost my *Athenaeum* cheque!" His harping on details of ill-health, his tedious explanations for lateness which having gone from the beginning to the end would then work backwards, were never alienating or aggressive in their quavering insistence, but as humourless as could be.

To turn from such earnest repetitions about a missed train to his terse masterly book-reviewing is to wonder at what stage the axe fell and left the striking economical thought stripped of wordiness. There is hardly a major poet or prose writer on whom he did not have his scholarly say. After his return to London in 1897 and the publication of *New Poems* his poetry-writing prac- tically ceased. But a mass of literary studies was produced, against all odds, by his tardy industry—that of someone who scrambles through a hedge rather than use the gate. He never started even, but to the difficulty inherent in any task was added that of high pressure, as an editor's telegram would confirm. The reason may have been the same as that of any other dilatory person; it may, in addition, be found in too general a sense of time.

I do not know [he wrote of himself] but that I live pretty well as much in the past and future as in the present, which seems a very little patch between the two. It has been more or less a habit through life; and during the last fifteen years, from the widened vantage of survey then gained, it has come to dominate my mental outlook. So that you might almost say, putting it hyperbolically, I view all mundane happenings with the Fall for one terminus and the Millenium for the other. If I want to gauge the significance of a contemporary event of any mark, I dump it down as near as I can in its proximate place between these boundaries. There it takes up very little room.

His literary judgments were not idiosyncratic; they contrived individuality within tradition—they broke old ground. Only one major writer was studied with a verdict divergent from the usual. Thompson conceded willingly that the *Pilgrim's Progress* having stood the test of two centuries was a work of immense vitality to men of all beliefs or no belief.

But as to Bunyan's imagination, we refuse to subscribe to tradition and Macaulay. He was a typical Saxon of the lower class, if a glorified type. He had vigour, forthrightness, narrative gift, a certain kind of vision, and ingenuity. But imagination he had not; a sound trotter, but no Pegasus. . . . We are told, indeed, of darkness and hideous sights, dreadful sounds, and the mouth of hell agape by the wayside. But there is no attempt to realise or suggest these terrors to the reader by a single touch of fancy or magic phrase, such as the great imaginative writers would have given us in a sentence or so. Hellmouth affects us less than an iron foundry, so poorly and barely is it rendered. . . . His Despair is a schoolboy's giant—a stupid billet-head clumping about with a cudgel, so rightly distrustful of his bacon-fed bucolic eloquence that he must reinforce it with sound thumps. In spite of his feudal castle, he is a farmer-like, domestic creature, of very honest orderly habits, and has a wife to counsel his dull brain. She is Diffidence. Despair taking counsel from Diffidence—the weaker passion strengthening the stronger! After cudgelling his prisoners, the absurd, ineffectual creation lumbers upstairs to his wife and bed. As if Despair could sleep! . . .

It is the immortal work of a true and most original allegory-maker—perhaps the best of allegory-makers. But it is not what it has hastily been called—a work of strong imagination, unless we are to use that word in a special and unauthentic sense.

Chesterton remarked that the shortest way of describing the Victorian age is to say that Francis Thompson stood outside it. But in his literary investigations he was not outside any age or school, ranging through different countries. Lives and men and faces are peered at too in these studies—yes, even faces, for he could scan and describe a portrait where he would not a living face. His last word about the man who in his early youth had got under his skin and remained there was as of one known better than had he been seen and heard.

A little, wrinkly, high-foreheaded, dress-as-you-please man; a meandering, inhumanly intellectual man, shy as a hermit-crab, and as given to shifting his lodgings; much enduring, inconceivable of way, sweet-hearted, fine-natured, small-spited, uncanny as a sprite begotten of libraries; some-thing of a bore to many, by reason of talking like a book in coat and breeches—undeniably clever and wonderful talk none the less; master of a great, unequal, seductive and irritating style; author of sixteen delightful and intolerable volumes, part of which can never die, and much of which can never live: that is De Quincey.

(To the reader already conscious of parallels between Thompson and his "very own Thomas De Quincey" a new detail seems almost humorously to clinch things—"given to shifting his lodgings.")

Of all this criticism, and that which enlarged itself into imaginative writing, as in his essay on Shelley, and of writing imaginative from the start, it may be said by those who admire him as a poet that he was as great a prose writer, little as he is known as such. The bulk is there to enforce the claim of quality, and a breadth of range as between sound reviewing and fantasy. In the latter genre, *Moestitiae Encomium* opens thus:

Marsh, and night. There are sounds; no man shall say what sounds. There are shadows; no man shall say what shadows.

There is light; were there not shadow, no man should call it light. The landscape is a sketch blotted in with smoke of Erebus, and greys from the cheek of death: those trees which threaten from the horizon—they are ranked apparitions, no boon of gracious God. The heaven is a blear copy of the land. Athwart the saturnine marsh, runs long, pitilessly straight, ghastly with an inward pallor (for no gleam dwells in it from the sky), the leprous, pined, infernal watercourse; a water for the Plutonian naiads—exhaling cold perturbation. It is a stream, a land, a heaven pernicious to the heart of man. Over this comes up of a sudden an unlawful moon. My very heart blanches. . . .

From such romanticism—as from anything else—to metaphysical thought was the easy step for him that it was for Patmore. *Health and Holiness: a Study of the Relations between Brother Ass the Body, and his Rider the Soul* would be after Patmore's own heart, and it is not too fantastic that he considered Thompson's prose better than his poetry—and, he added, that his talk was better than his prose. "It is good news that you are writing prose," he once wrote to him. "You know how perfectly great I think what I have read of your prose. After all, the greatest things must be said in prose."

XI

I F Meynell thought he was able to stand between Thompson and disaster he was sometimes made less certain of it. Thompson had bed, board, and work, and rarely let more than a day or two pass without knocking at the door in Palace Court. But within himself he periodically reached a crisis of fatality, for which, it will be seen, he raked in the material from far and near.

28 Elgin Avenue.
July 19, 1900.

Dear Wilfrid,

I designed to call in on Wednesday, but was sick with a horrible journey on the underground. Yesterday again I intended, & again was sick & exhausted for like reason. Today, though better, I am still not well. I hope I may manage tomorrow. I have been full of worry, depression, and unconquerable foreboding. The other day, as I was walking outside my lodgings, steeped in ominous thoughts, a tiny child began to sing beside me in her baby voice, over and over repeated:

"O danger, O danger,
O danger is coming near."

My heart sank, and I almost trembled with fear.

There was every reason for sinking of heart, outside my own gloomy affairs. My prophecies of foreign complications in the East, and universal war, are drawing nearer and nearer to fulfilment. Small-pox has broken out in West Kensington, & at that time (I have no later news) was spreading rapidly. Disaster was, and is, drawing downwards over the whole horizon. And I feel my private fate involved in it. I am oppressed with fatality. . . .

Oh, that I were a *man* again! I must, I cannot help but go if things do not soon turn. Were it not for the power my love of you gives you over me, it is not the fear of consequences would have kept me back. This time, it would be mercifully short. I have neither ye latent stubbornness of constitution, nor ye latent belief in a destiny, which made it so tough a strife before. The very streets weigh upon me. These horrible streets, with their gangrenous multitudes, blackening ever into lower mortifications of humanity! The brute men; these lads who have almost lost the faculty of human speech, who howl & growl like animals, or use a tongue which is itself a cancerous disintegration of speech: these girls whose practice is a putrid ulceration of love, venting foul and purulent discharge—for their very utterance is hideous blasphemy against the sacrosanctity of lovers' language! Nothing but the vocabulary of the hospital, images of corruption and fleshly ruin, can express the objects offered to eye and ear in these loathsome streets. The air is fulsome with its surcharge of tainted humanity. We lament the smoke of London:—it were nothing without the fumes of congregated evil, the herded effluence from millions of festering souls. At times I am merely sick with it.

But all this baby-wail is useless, and worthy of the baby I am become. Good-bye, dear Wilfrid, till I see you; which I will manage on Friday, whatever comes, short of actual illness.

Yours ever,

F. T.

Wilfrid Whitten of the *Academy* remarked that in these later years Thompson suffered more from the possession of money than from the lack of it. That was to presume it certain that prosperity led more than poverty to laudanum-taking. Meynell no doubt shared that view somewhat, and Thompson in fact lived within a narrow margin of subsistence. Sometimes through Meynell's mere forgetfulness a landlady's bill would remain unpaid, buried no doubt on his library table; at other times he simply lacked the money with which to pay it, and Thompson would be harried at his lodging for a more regular arrangement. Even so, situations were saved which he thought irredeemable. "You were right," he wrote. "Mrs. Maries has given way, on the understanding that you will make some arrangement with her before the end of the month." But behind the scenes of the poet's life, concealed by the thin curtain of not-cruel circumstances, his nature was running its own downward course in its own time. He had only now entered his forties, but he knew in both body and spirit that it was a late hour, and when things went amiss he had a despairing man's instinct to make bad worse.

I trust Hind's article will go to him tonight [he wrote to Meynell] and then I shall have done what I can. God help me in the struggle which now begins, for I see the conditions will be much harder than before, and I have reason to dread the worst. God bless and thank you and yours, dear Wilfrid, for your long and heroic kindness to me. And remember if ever you want to communicate with me, the *Poste Restante* Charing Cross will find me. I shall make a point of going there every now and then, in case such an occasion should arise.

Ever and in all fates yours,
Francis Thompson

These crises, arising only at long intervals from incidents now lost in obscurity, were cured but not prevented. It is clear that his journalistic efforts were becoming too burdensome. The editorship of the *Academy* passed out of Hind's hands into those of Teignmouth Shore. "The interview last Friday," Thompson wrote to Meynell, absent for a few days, "landed me on a doubtfully hospitable Shore. All articles to be cut down to a column. Immediate result, fifteen shillings for this week. Since, I have received more books, bringing it up to ye usual 30 shillings. But takes 5 books & 5 articles to reach this result—all to be done by tomorrow. Don't know what to do . . . therefore am waiting most anxiously for your return." At such a rate of pay this was hard going, and would need a fit and energetic man; and it would have been unlike Meynell not to realize it. "Things have become impossible," wrote Thompson. "B. did not outright refuse me an advance on my poem, but told me to call again and 'talk it over.' . . . The only thing is for me to relieve you of my burden— at any rate for the present—and go back whence I came. There will be no danger in my present time of life and outworn strength that I should share poor Coventry's complaint (that of outliving his ambition to live)." He had sometimes a suspicion of difficulties for his friend. "To have to talk of money-matters to you is itself a misery, a sordidness. How much worse in its way all this must press on you is comprehensible to anyone. We are no longer as we were ten years ago. You have grown-up children to launch in life."

He had indeed. And in this very fact that the elder children were now growing up there was a brightening of the horizon for Thompson.

The eldest daughter Monica had always been much beloved by him, and now on her engagement in 1903 he wrote assuring her of an

affection which you once—so long since—purchased with a poppy in that Friston field. "Keep it," you said (though you have doubtless forgotten) "as long as you live." I have kept it, and with it I keep you, my dearest. I do not say or show much, for I am an old man compared with you, and no companion for your young life. But never, my dear, doubt I love you. And if I have the chance to show it I will do. I am ill at saying all I doubtless should say to a young girl on her engagement. I have no experience in it, my Monica. I can only say I love you; and if there is any kind or tender thing I should have said, believe it is in my heart, though it be not here.

Then from a tea shop in Westbourne Grove, where he repaired after mis-timing the marriage ceremony at the nearby church by arriving too early and leaving in the belief that he was too late, he wrote:

You were a prophetess (though you needed not be a sybil to foretell my tricks and manners). I reached the church just ten minutes after twelve, to find vacancy, as you had fore-warned me. A young lady that might have been yourself approached the church by the back entrance just as I came away, but on inspection she had no trace of poppy-land. So I can only wish by letter you and your husband all the happiness God can imagine for you. It seems but the other day, my dearest sister (may I not call you so? For you are all to me as younger sisters and brothers—to me who have long ceased practically to have any

166

sisters of my own) that you were a child with me at Friston, and I myself still very much of a child. Now the time is come I foresaw then,—"knowing well when some few days are over, You vanish from me to another." You may pardon me if I feel a little sadness, even while I am glad for your gladness, my dear.

But it was with another of the grown-up members of the family that Thompson was forming a bond of affection and common interest which for a few years was actually a compensating sweetness for the decline that time was working in him.

Everard was the Meynells' second son, a very young art student at the Slade School, bearded at nineteen, and with a dark glow of personality like a young figure out of Giorgione. His early development and many-sidedness made his short life a full one. He was reserved, only his actions speaking of his mind's processes; his love of the poets was almost furtive, so unobtrusively did he establish familiarity with them—a familiarity which came to include knowledge of editions, dates, types, and bindings, especially of the books of the sixteenth- and seventeenth-century poets. It was an instance of a flair—expertness which seems to arrive overnight. Everard was also a beginner in journalism and authorship. He left the Slade. His diversity of interests focussed on an unexpected enterprise; he became a bookseller.

The Serendipity[1] Shop was situated first in the semi-retirement of a passage-like approach at one end of Westbourne Grove. In subsequent quarters at Museum Street and then in Shepherd's Market in Mayfair it gained a modest but world-wide reputation, and a backward glance now at one or other of its "catalogues of rare books," where Donne first editions were modestly priced, and such a treasure as Herrick's *Hesperides* of 1648 is a "very fine copy," explains collectors' enthusiasm for this stock, acquired without capital and by means of the knowledge in which devotion seems a substitute for experience.

It was the Westbourne Grove Serendipity Shop which in

[1] A word coined by Horace Walpole, from the *Arabian Nights* story of the Princes of Serendip (ancient name of Ceylon) whose adventures led them to unexpected discoveries. Serendipity is therefore the finding of a treasure when looking for something else.

these early nineteen-hundreds Thompson added to Palace Court as a place of constant call; it was on his route to almost anywhere, and there were several reasons why it would become urgent to have a word with the young shopman. The most unlikely, and one of the most frequent, of these was cricket. "If ever a figure," E. V. Lucas wrote once, "seemed to say, 'Take me anywhere in the world so long as it is not to a cricket match,' that figure was Francis Thompson's. And his eye supported it. His eye had no brightness: it swung laboriously upon its object; whereas the enthusiasts of St. John's Wood dart their glances like birds. But Francis Thompson was born to baffle the glib inference." So Thompson had a cricket sense, and his following of the course of a cricket season was a definite distraction from the woes of life, which it is welcome to think of in looking back on his days; and he maintained a general idea of the place and form of the counties even if his newspaper was often only the newsboy's placard.

It had begun of course in boyhood, a passion shared then by his sisters. (After she had been thirty years a nun one sister could still remember seven names out of a Lancashire eleven in a crucial match.) Living for some years within reach of the Old Trafford ground Thompson as a youth had his gods among the Lancashire team; and of the memorable match against Gloucestershire in 1878 when Hornby and Barlow pulled the game out of the fire for Lancashire, a feat witnessed by him at the age of eighteen, he wrote in later years the nostalgic cricket verses which have become part of the literature of the game, beginning

It is little I repair to the matches of the Southron folk,
    Though my own red roses there may blow;
It is little I repair to the matches of the Southron folk,
    Though the red roses crest the caps, I know.
For the field is full of shades as I near the shadowy coast,
And a ghostly batsman plays to the bowling of a ghost,
And I look through my tears on a soundless-clapping host
    As the run-stealers flicker to and fro,
        To and fro:—
    O my Hornby and my Barlow long ago!

168

It was true that the days were now over for passing through the turnstiles. Many plans were made to do so which never came off. He was deterred by some well-sounding reason from what he had only thought he meant to do. "I did not go to Lords," he wrote to his fellow enthusiast Everard. "Could not get there before lunch; & getting a paper at Baker Street saw Lancashire had collapsed and Middlesex were in again. So turned back without getting my ticket—luckily kept from another disappointing day." For in Everard he had the crony which the cricket supporter needs—better still, the opponent. For the sake of argument Everard was for Yorkshire—or, rather, he was for Yorkshire and the pleasure of argument ensued. Of a match lost by Lancashire in 1905 Thompson wrote magnanimously: "Well done, Yorkshire! your county is coming up hand over hand I see by the placards. I said how it would be, so I am not surprised. Our tail is not plucky. Love to all, dear Ev.—F. T." In another cricket letter Thompson makes reference to his own idea that he had a physical resemblance to certain members of reigning families.

Dear Ev.,

Character counts, even in cricket. This morning I was looking at a *Daily Mail* photo of the South African team for the coming cricket season. One of the faces instantly caught my eye. "Well!" said I, "if character count for anything in cricket, this should be the bowler they say has the Bosanquet style." Since Hall Caine is no Shakespeare, Plonplon no soldier, & neither ye Tsar nor ye Prince of Wales [George V] are Thompsonian poets, great was my surprise when I found the fellow *was* the Bosanquet bowler.

Behind the Serendipity Shop in a large studio the bookseller generally had a painting on hand, and Thompson sat for him; and amid the paraphernalia of Everard's many enterprises—for in this pastime business he could introduce almost all his likings, and he varied the shop's contents with Hollar engravings,

169

Japanese books and prints, Mrs. Cameron photographs, Eric Gill woodcuts and statuettes, drawings and etchings by contemporary artists there was the clay outfit for mask-taking, and it was there that he took a life-mask of Thompson's head and hand.

He had another small function in regard to the poet. Wilfrid Meynell's connection with the publishing firm of Burns and Oates had constantly increased as his usefulness was proved in his business faculty, and pioneer work in good book production. And as Thompson's interests must be served in any concern in which he had a hand, Meynell arranged that he should be commissioned to write a life of St. Ignatius Loyola—a plan to give him employment without the strain and stress of book-reviewing to time. In order to space out the money he was to receive, payment for the work was made piecemeal, at the rate of a pound for every three pages delivered; and Everard's shop was handy for the reception of the MS. and the pay-out. What characterized all these dealings between Thompson and the mature young man twenty years his junior was the quiet affectionate wit which was Everard's idiom, and at which, as it was probably aimed against some cherished anxiety or vociferated excuse of Thompson's, he could not at once smile—until slowly, unwillingly, the smile had to break, and there is no more mirthful smile in the world than the reluctant one which is yet irrepressible, as Thompson's with Everard.

During these years when Thompson's flow of poetry had ceased, resulting in inner destitution and desolation, he had at least some consciousness of past achievement; a body of evidence for it remained when all the condemnation was allowed for. With the publication of *New Poems* he had written: "Though my aims are unfulfilled, my place insecure, many things warn me that with this volume I am probably closing my brief poetic career." But unfulfilment was a comparative term, and the very reason for his suffering under his present dearth was that he knew he had proved his faculty. Some lines addressed to Meynell express his lament:

Ah, gone the days when for undying kindness
I still could render you undying song!
You yet can give, but I can give no more;
Fate, in her extreme blindness,
Has wrought me so great wrong.
I am left poor indeed;
Gone is my sole and amends-making store,
And I am needy with a double need.

Behold that I am like a fountained nymph,
Lacking her customed lymph,
The longing parched in stone upon her mouth,
Unwatered by its ancient plenty. She
(Remembering her irrevocable streams),
A Thirst made marble, sits perpetually
With sundered lips of still-memorial drouth.

But as for Wilfrid Meynell, the delight and the surprise of
Thompson's poetry did not demand refreshing; it was as new as
ever. What he coveted was recognition for what Thompson had
already done. And he could not conceive how he could do anyone
a greater favour than by an introduction to this poetry. It had
become his very terms of intercourse with his friends. Two
American men visiting Palace Court for the first time one night,
who had fared badly at the dinner table—for the climate of the
meals was variable and could fail deplorably when fair conditions
were most desirable, and the claret at 9d. a bottle to be had con-
veniently at *Maison Bourron* close by in Richmond Road was not
always provided—these Americans must have been hopeful when
before their departure Meynell beckoned them to follow him
into the library for "a special treat"—which however proved to
be the reading aloud of "The Hound of Heaven."

In due time Meynell was made the managing director of
Burns and Oates, and he attended at Orchard Street every day.
The premises there consisted of a long and narrow building of four
stories at the corner of Orchard Street and Granville Place; the
ground floor was the church-furnishing and Catholic book shop;

the first, the firm's offices; and the second, third, and fourth were uneconomical store-rooms until Meynell hit on a different idea for them and they were made into flats. These under his supervision —who was ingenious at the game and enjoyed it—were well designed and provided a long-shaped drawing-room, a dining-room, and five bedrooms and dressing-room. The top flat, with its long narrow white passage, skylights and round windows like portholes, had a ship-like appearance. The address was 2A Granville Place. The whole building has now disappeared.

The older of the young Meynells had begun to disperse, and the Palace Court house was big.

The home in which a young family has grown up from infancy is the most settled of homes, and to leave it seems like putting aside too much. But in the little green horse-omnibus between Palace Court and Orchard Street, Meynell was losing an hour or two a day, and finally a move was decided on. Flat-living had not then become London's way of life, and if Alice Meynell, to whom it came naturally to preserve some kind of dignity of circumstance or frugal elegance, was slightly surprised to find herself leaving the house she loved for cabin-like quarters to be reached only by climbing seventy-odd stone steps, she yet preserved a characteristic belief that the decision was in infallible hands.

For Thompson the removal of the family to a greater distance was not disastrous. Street-geography had been born in him once and for all when streets had been his home. So had his exposure of himself to all weathers. No one could be more devastated by cold, but evasion of it had never been practical. A letter to the child Monica, written one Christmas Eve, illustrates how a tramp of a mile or two between Elgin Avenue and Palace Court on a cold wet night, which most men would reject in favour of an armchair, was by him taken for granted. "I have just come home after a fruitless attempt to get in at any rate the most part of my work before Xmas, very cold & wet & tired. I shall see you at any rate tomorrow night, I trust. I must run up with these notes for you & your father before I go to bed, since I want you to have them on Xmas morning, & I am too late for ye post. This weather crumples me up." So Granville Place was negotiable for him, though it might emphasize his unpunctuality. "Francis Thompson has just arrived," wrote Alice Meynell to an absent member of the family, "at about eight-thirty to the seven o'clock dinner, or rather to the one-thirty luncheon, for that was the meal he chose, as he was going to confession tonight. I think it is the same confession that kept him many moons ago."

This move was in 1905. But at the end of that year it again became evident that the London winter was injurious to Thompson, and again it was to the Franciscans, who never missed an opportunity to show their affection for this fellow spirit, that Meynell turned. Thompson was to lodge near the monastery at Crawley in Sussex.

XII

"**I** FEEL depressed at going away from you all—it seems like a breaking with my past, the beginning of I know not what change, or what doubtful future," Thompson wrote to Everard, and proceeded to elaborate this reluctance to go to Crawley.

Change *as* change is always hateful to me; yet my life has been changeful enough in various ways. And I have noticed these changes always come in shocks & crises after a prolonged period of monotony. In my youth I sighed against monotony, & wanted romance; now I dread romance. Romance is romantic only for the hearers & onlookers, not for the actors. It is hard to enter its gates (happily) but to repass them is impossible. Once step aside from the ways of "comfortable men," you cannot regain them. You will live & die under the law of the intolerable thing they call romance. Though it may return on you only in cycles & crises, you are ever dreading its next manifestation. Nor need you be "romantic" to others; the most terrible romances are inward, & the intolerableness of them is that they pass in silence. One person told me that my own life was a beautiful romance. "Beautiful" is not my standpoint. The sole beautiful romances are the Saints', which are essentially inward. But I never meant to write all this.

And again, when he arrived, to Everard: "I am a helpless waterlogged & dismasted vessel, drifting without power to guide my own course, & equally far from port whichever way I turn my eyes. I can only fling this bottle into the sea & leave you to discern my impotent & wrecked condition."

The Capuchins' general welcome had often been expressed in notes from Father Anselm. "How I long for a return of the happy days at Pantasaph, when we discussed all things in heaven and on

174

earth and in infernis." And Thompson too must have longed for those days of comparative vigour when he walked on the Welsh hills. For now he wrote to Meynell in January: "I just manage to get on when it's not cold, & have a horrible time when it is. I get better food than I ever had in lodgings since Storrington, & keep shut up in a nice warm room, or else—but for these things—I should go to pieces. O for Spring! & not ye fraudulent substitute which of late years has been rather worse than winter."

Existence was now a narrowing of even his slight contact with the world about him, the automatic solitude of one from whom life is falling away. But within this restricted existence small circumstances loomed large; his over-sensitized nervous system made him start at any sudden sound, and tremble with forebodings, and he lacked the will or the energy reasonably to leave his bed, and was exacerbated by well-intentioned interference. At the beginning of April, 1906, in what must have been a late season, he was still at Crawley, and wrote:

> c/o Mrs. Gravely,
> 11 Victoria Road, Crawley, Sussex.
> Tuesday.

Dear Wilfrid,

. . . I understand that Madam had written you that I am very ill, & must go into hospital or see a doctor at once.

It is all baseless nonsense. I told you in my last letter how I was, & am like to be till Spring relieves me. But I am, thank God, far from being as bad as I was in London last winter, & should have been again, or rather worse, had I been exposed to ye conditions of my life in London & its horrible fogs & smoke, which are killing to me.

The whole trouble is simply about my lying late in bed, which, as you know, has nothing to do with illness, & was a difficulty at Pantasaph as it is here. If that were removed my landlady has no objection (she says) to keep me. I have arranged, therefore, that she shall try coming into my room in a morning & making sure that I am really wakened. She has agreed to try that plan for a month longer, & if it succeed in getting me up, she will then not object to my staying on, she says. Here is the whole substance & extent of the matter. I do not doubt of ye plan succeeding. For the bother is just that I answer automatically to ye call at my door, without really waking. My landlady declared that she never meant to say she wanted me to go; but only to represent that she could not go on under ye inconvenience of my late rising. . . .

The letter then says all this over again at length. A further eighth sheet adds: "Wednesday. This was too late to go last night: so I add a line this morning. We put ye new plan in practice this morning, and it got me up *instanter*—I knew it would, from past experience."

With the coming of better weather he returned to London. It was the return, too, to a more settled habit of laudanum-taking, the medicine which he administered to his increased ills. A doctor later expressed the opinion that it was with opium that Thompson had kept himself alive in his last year or two. At what point a moral judgment comes in, as regards what would also at times destroy his consciousness, it would take some rigid rule-maker to know. Alice Meynell called him deliberately "one of the most innocent of men," and not a person who remembers that gentle, guileless, sensitive fragment of life could disagree. Coleridge said of himself that he was "seduced to the accursed habit ignorantly," and he affirmed that his "sole sensuality was not to be in pain." What arguments of self-accusation and defence—awake and suffering, or easeful and sleepy—might occupy Thompson were hidden in silence on a subject pervaded by its own oblivion. In whatever way he resolved or left unresolved the ethical problem of his own habit, he had the normal judgment of the effect of that habit in others. In fact in writing of Coleridge he so much exaggerates those effects that he may have been offering himself a reminder. He belittles Coleridge in order to enlarge the Coleridge catastrophe. He writes:

Then came ill-health and opium. Laudanum by the wine-glassful and half-pint at a time soon reduced him to the journalist-lecturer and philosopher, who projected all things, executed nothing; only the eloquent tongue left. So he perished—the

176

mightiest intellect of the day, and great was the fall thereof. There remain of him his poems, and a quantity of letters painful to read. They show him wordy, full of weak lamentation, deplorably feminine and strengthless.

The sometimes flushed and dozing man who visited the Meynells at the Granville Place flat was suspected of some return to his old enslavement, but during all these years he had on the whole established his ability to manage his own frugal, behind-hand, barren, industrious life in his own way, and not without the fitful use of laudanum. The account sent by a chemist in Harrow Road is: "To Laudanum supplied from Dec. 24th/04 to Feb. 28th/05," and its items are "7 lots @ 10d. & 1 lot @ 6d.," for the total of six shillings and fourpence. One of his notebooks shows that on the amount consumed he kept at any rate temporarily the watchfulness which is an attempt at self-discipline.

Friday 1 bot.	$= 2\frac{1}{2}$
Saturday 1	$= 2\frac{1}{2}$
Sunday (1, 1, 1) 3	$= 7\frac{1}{2}$
Monday 2	$= 5$
Tuesday 2	$= 5$
Thursday, 1	$= 2\frac{1}{2}$

Laudanum was cheap. To pay Thompson's landlady direct, and to be unlavish in supplying him with pocket money was diplomatic, but no water-tight measure; and extra shillings, of which it was intended to deprive him, his laudanum-need taught him how to secure for himself. A few pawn tickets lying with the chemist's bill among his papers indicate the relation between the two; they had got him three shillings on a "Jacket-vest," one on a shirt, one on trousers, and two shillings and sixpence on a "Silver medal."

He was not reduced to the misery of idleness for he still did some reviewing for the *Athenaeum*; its editor Vernon Rendall treated him with extraordinary consideration, writing to him at Crawley: "I am very sorry to hear of your illness, which may have been aggravated I fear by our clerks. I will try to make them send things correctly in future. Do not hurry now about anything you have. You are sure to be in need of rest and recreation. . . ," He had also the Burns and Oates commission, which took him often to the British Museum reading-room for books on his subject, and which progressed in due stages, as St. Ignatius continued to keep this strange company.

But the time came, in the summer of 1907, when a marked deterioration was evident in his excessive thinness and lethargy, and this time it was to Wilfrid Blunt that Meynell turned for country quarters and friendly company. Thompson agreed willingly one evening to the plan, but on the next the reluctance that is born in the night, searching for an impediment, found one in his clothing. When this was supplemented with a supply of new shirts and with new boots, and when it was promised that Everard Meynell should accompany him and stay for a few days he had no wish to resist, and on the 24th of August Meynell and his son called for him by arrangement at eleven o'clock. They expected to wait while he rose from his bed. They found the bed empty and Thompson vanished. When they had waited, wondering, he came in. With the unexpected importance he attached to some of the details of living, harping on them earnestly, he had been some distance to obtain the special brand of pork-pie he believed in, for sustenance on the journey.

If health and life had depended on favourable conditions, Thompson would have improved when brought within the radius of Blunt's way of life. At Newbuildings Place, with its unique character of being highly civilized and a little wild; its English homeliness in a region of small oaks, combined with far-fetched attar roses from Damascus and Arab horses in the paddock; peacocks strutting or perched on wood-stacks; estate farms and cottages with Sussex peasant tenants of a squire clothed in a Bedouin robe, who as host to many visitors was both casual and concerned, and whose aesthetic art of life could not go wrong— this would have made a pleasant place in which to regain a hold on life. Thompson and Everard were housed in a cottage on the estate, used chiefly for guests, and Everard should have had full satisfaction in seeing the poet lapped in the luxury of the mere essentials of life, made beautiful for him in the bright flames of the log fires; but instead he wrote to Grazia Carbone, his future wife:

> I have just boiled the poet's eggs & toasted his cakes, which I hear him eating inside. He is very grateful for what I do for him, but he is so used to the very sorry comforts of his town existence that he has taken a little while to get into the way of being here. As it is, he never looks across the lovely landscapes, never goes out into the beautiful green spaces all round our cottage, & altogether presents a pitiable country figure. It is strange to see him twisting his moustache & pulling down his cuffs when Mr. Blunt approaches, as if that could make him look less of a wreck, & it is strange to observe that he fancies he cuts quite a good figure, while beside the great healthy bulk of W. S. B. he looks too thin to be alive.

In the cottage's candlelight when he went to bed at night he lay propped up with pillows, his prayer-book in his hand. When Everard returned to London and his Serendipity Shop, Blunt proposed that Thompson should be moved to another cottage half a mile away, to be in the devoted care of one of Blunt's servants and his wife. Meynell wrote to Blunt: "I think the proposition about a room under David's roof as wise as it is kind. If you spoke of it to Thompson as an arranged thing, sparing him the mental effort of making up his mind, I believe he would fall in with it. I shall be very anxious to hear how he seems." From his new quarters at "Rascal's Corner," Thompson was driven every day to Newbuildings for luncheon and tea with Blunt, until his increased weakness made the arrangement irregular. It was during this time that Neville Lytton, Blunt's son-in-law, made the drawing of Thompson now in the National Portrait Gallery.

These are extracts from Blunt's *Diaries* at the time:

> 26th Aug. Thompson is distinctly better today. I fetched him down from Gosbrook in the phaeton, and had a long talk with him after luncheon. We first got into touch with each

other over a common hatred of European civilization and the destruction wrought by it on all that was beautiful in the world, the destruction of happiness, of the happier races by the less happy, and so gradually to the despair of the intellectual part of mankind with what life gave, and the craving for a life after death. I gave him something of my view and asked him abruptly what his own view was. He said, "Oh, about that I am entirely orthodox; indeed, it is my only consolation." This led to a question about his Catholic bringing-up, and he told me that he was a Catholic born, both his parents having been, however, converts. . . . It was a mistake to suppose his father had treated him harshly. . . . If he had spoken openly to his father telling him how repugnant the details of doctoring were to him, he would not have insisted, but as he did not speak his father did not know, and he acquiesced in what was arranged for him. His repugnance was a physical one which he could not overcome. . . . "As a boy of seventeen," he said, "I was incredibly vain; it makes me blush now to remember what I thought of myself. Neither my father nor my mother had the least appreciation of literary things or the least suspicion that I had any talent of that kind, but I was devoured with literary ambition; all my medical studies were wasted because I would not work, but ran off from my classes to the libraries to read. If my father had known he would not have forced me to go on."

12th Sept. Thompson goes on in a half alive state at David's, apparently content with an existence purely negative. He takes laudanum, David reports, daily, and sleeps at night with a stertorous sound. At noon every day I send a vehicle for him, and he joins us here at luncheon, very feeble and quite silent, except it be on some very trivial subject. He seems incapable of bringing his mind to bear on any complex thought, and sits through the afternoon with a volume of *Martin Chuzzlewit*, sometimes held upside down in his hand, which he does not read, nodding, and three parts asleep, like a very aged man. He seems happy, however, and I do not disturb him.

Blunt, who was himself subject to attacks of severe illness, had a trained nurse in residence at Newbuildings—the mild-eyed Miss Lawrence, who had become Blunt's second self in the carrying-

FRANCIS THOMPSON
Painting by Everard Meynell, about 1906

EVERARD MEYNELL

out of his practical goodness. In September she could write semi-reassuringly to Wilfrid Meynell: "Mr. Blunt paid Mr. Thompson a long visit last evening, and I hear to-day that he is better. He told Mr. Blunt that he will stay here for the present. The doctor is going to see him again. Mr. Thompson liked him, which is something gained. Mr. Thompson has not come to-day, but we have sent twice, and the boy will enquire again this evening." And Blunt wrote to Meynell, also in September: "I shall be very glad to keep Thompson on here as long as the weather continues fine. The stay is doing him good & he managed to finish an article for the *Athenaeum* yesterday. We don't see much of him but he is well looked after by David's wife. All the same, when the weather breaks he will probably be better back in London."

But as the weeks went by Blunt saw in Thompson "a poor frail spirit; in a body terrible in its emaciation, a mere shred of humanity, fading visibly into the eternal shadow. As he moved among us, or lay silent in his dreams, his face might have been that of some Spanish saint of the days of Isabel the Catholic, tortured to inanition by his own austerities; or again, it might, so small it was, have been that of a prematurely aged & dying child." They were weeks of beautiful weather which prolonged the summer into October. But on the 14th of that month Blunt wrote to Meynell: "I am not satisfied about Thompson, and should be glad to get him back safe to London. So don't put off sending Everard for him. He seems quite given up to laudanum now, & I feel anxious lest he shd. have some sudden break down or break up."

When a measure fails of which much has been hoped, hope fastens on a reversion to the original conditions, and Meynell now believed that, near him, Thompson might be happier and better. He was not at all prepared for any distinct change. Everard Meynell even wrote to Blunt: "I propose calling for Francis on Wednesday. I will first look in at Rascal's Corner in the morning and then walk up to Newbuildings. I suppose I will bear back an extraordinarily stronger person than the lamentable poet we brought down to you." It was far otherwise.

In Thompson's present state the smallest incidents of life were shattering, and when an umbrella fell against him in the railway carriage he said brokenly: "I am the target of all disaster." When Wilfrid Meynell saw him he was aghast, and Everard wrote to his betrothed: "I am just back from Newbuildings bearing with me the skeleton of F. T." They knew too well now about the laudanum but it had yet to be brought into the open. Everard writes again: "Father went to F. T.'s lodgings yesterday and found him so ill that he asked him openly what was the matter, at which poor Francis after his years of concealment said: 'Wilfrid, it is laudanum poisoning. I put myself in your hands.' "

Meynell asked him if he would go into hospital, and the Hospital of St. John and St. Elizabeth took him into its care on November 1. Everard wrote to Grazia Carbone on November 5: "I saw the poet who has entered into the spirit of his cure admirably. Imagine, he weighs only 5 stone."

But he was in fact dying from tuberculosis of the lungs. He lay in the hospital for twelve days. He was given the laudanum which was keeping him alive. His only visible distress during these days was when the time for the dose drew near and the need for it had set up its inward clamour. A nun nursed him with the care and love of her double vocation.

He read W. W. Jacobs's *Many Cargoes,* and his prayer-book. When Meynell sat by his bed Thompson wished to hold his hand. A priest ministered to him before he died at dawn on November 13, 1907. He was forty-eight years old. He was buried in St. Mary's Cemetery, Kensal Green.

Meynell wept for his friend. It was a multifold tie that was ended, and it made a break in his life.

Thompson's career had been in almost all respects the antithesis to his own. Meynell wrote verse throughout his long life, but he did not imagine that therein lay his long service to literature. His true convinced approach to literature was through the service of poetry in others—and most of all in Thompson.

In this as in all else he was the good giver who is averse from thanks or recognition. Thompson was what it is only less difficult to be—a good taker. He had poetry, but he had no other worldly possession; for nineteen years he found himself under continuous obligation to a man who had everything else—a singularly lovely marriage, devoted children, influence, health, a wide variety of friends and interests, and a general compelling effectiveness. One conceivable conflict had never arisen. In Thompson's love of Alice Meynell, Meynell found no reason for distress, and Thompson no cause for elation. It was never an issue between them, because it was never an issue between Thompson and Alice Meynell herself. She read his poems of love, and spoke of them to others, as pieces of literature, remote from her own personality.

The text-books say that such a situation of having and not-having, of control and dependence, should have produced discontent and discord in the relationship of the two men. It produced tolerance and trust. The relation between them was mostly an inexpressive one, of the kind in which sheer ease and intimacy are not the least precious part. It was a relation so simple and altogether untortured as to afford no field of investigation for the analytically-minded of the present day.

Thompson, it is true, had enjoyed his occasional grumble to Patmore. "That was a very absurd and annoying situation in which I was placed by W. M.'s curious handling of me . . ." (page 95). And again: "This should have been my second book if W. M. had not frustrated my careful waiting by committing me to ye publication of my ill-starred volume . . ." (page 126). For to Patmore he was not above a little showing-off of his own would-be independence, his pathetically non-existent man-of-the-worldliness—as also in making his fruitless boast of his social success with Katie King in 1893: ". . . a girl I met here wants me to visit her, which is pretty fair for the very evening one reaches town."

But the more cogent of the "documents in the case" are otherwise, as in Thompson's letter to Meynell in 1900 when a

mood of despair had almost taken him back to the streets:
"Were it not for the power my love of you gives you over me,
it is not the fear of consequences would have kept me back." And
again the truth is in the lines he addressed to Meynell:

O tree of many branches! One thou hast
Thou barest not, but grafted'st on thee. Now,
Should all men's thunders break on thee, and leave
Thee reft of bough and blossom, that one branch
Shall cling to thee, my Father, Brother, Friend,
Shall cling to thee, until the end of end.

Above all there had been the persistent background of intercourse
and encouragement, given and sought, of Sutherland Avenue
landladies and Fleet Street editors jointly cajoled; of laudanum
and health "cures" organized and undertaken; of house and
children made free to him as if he were a son of the first and elder
brother of the others. Only in one thing was there a seeming
failure of intimacy; but perhaps it was a deeper intimacy on both
sides. Thompson between 1888 and 1907 never told Meynell the
painful and paining truth that he had seriously relapsed into
laudanum-taking; Meynell never asked what he might have
been afraid to hear answered. At this level they spoke to each
other with silence.

A unique relationship was finished. And yet a poet leaves so
much behind him that there was still the chance for his friend to
act those parts towards his poetry which he had performed for
Thompson himself. And from now for the rest of his life Meynell
had the happiness of serving the interest of Thompson's work.

His reputation had increased of late years as it were causelessly.
The sale of his *New Poems* had been negligible, and no book had
appeared since; the personal obscurity of his life would make it
unknown whether he were alive or dead; but no doubt because
the outstanding praise of a few critics had made a more lasting
sound than the distaste of others, his reputation had been like the
growth which goes on while one sleeps—the reputation, that is,
of his writing only, for it was like poetry without a poet. To
perpetuate this fame, and increase it, was Meynell's desire; he did

not then conceive to what an extent it would develop, though he wrote to Blunt soon after Thompson's death:

Our Thompson "on the town" is a strange apotheosis: the halfpenny press denounces the man who doesn't admire him! I heard from the Poet Laureate[1] this morning who defines what great poetry is, laments Thompson's failure to attain it, & concludes with the pious prayer: "May he rest in peace—from the critics!" But it is not Thompson who is perturbed by the critics.

The immediate need was to correct the impression, now getting into print, that the man who had died had led the furtive life of a degenerate, that he was "like Verlaine, a poet of sin"; that he must "have said, 'I will eat of all the fruits in the Garden of life,' and in the very satisfaction of his desire found its insatiableness." (The *Mercure de France* said that "he went mad and death happily put an end to his miseries.") This idea of the moral atmosphere being lifted through his death was the drawing of too-easy conclusions from his original vagrancy, rumours of opium, and from the secluded life he led as a matter of temperament. Even in his poetry evidence was found that he was a confessed evil-doer. "The Hound of Heaven," which for the coming generations was to be the religious poem of modern times best expressing the divine love—was it not a declaration of sinfulness?

> I fled Him down the nights and down the days;
>   I fled Him, down the arches of the years;
> I fled Him, down the labyrinthine ways
>   Of my own mind; and in the mist of tears
> I hid from Him, and under running laughter . . .

> Across the margent of the world I fled,
>   And troubled the gold gateways of the stars,
>   Smiting for shelter on their clangèd bars;
>   Fretted to dulcet jars
> And silvern chatter the pale ports o' the moon.
> I said to Dawn: Be sudden—to Eve: Be soon;
>   With thy young skiey blossoms heap me over
>   From this tremendous Lover. . . .

---

[1] Alfred Austin.

In fact, a drama of sin would be a cheap one beside this drama of love. But then in the poem the poet himself is called "Of all man's clotted clay the dingiest clot." Could the sin-theorist not point to that? Instead, he should discover that it was still within this drama of love that Thompson was so describing himself. He had always considered himself no object for human love; this was the dinginess which divine love could ignore in addressing him thus:

"All which I took from thee I did but take,
    Not for thy harms,
But just that thou might'st seek it in My arms.
    All which thy child's mistake
Fancies as lost, I have stored for thee at home:
    Rise, clasp My hand, and come!"

    Halts by me that footfall:
    Is my gloom, after all,
Shade of His hand, outstretched caressingly?
    "Ah, fondest, blindest, weakest,
    I am He whom thou seekest!
Thou dravest love from thee, who dravest Me."

For those who knew Thompson the reality of his life was in too sharp contrast with the fable. To correct the illusion, it was unnecessary to go into the habits of simple piety which are sometimes discarded with youth but were retained by him in maturity. (There was nothing merely ornamental about his starting a poem with the sign of the cross at the head of the paper or with the letters A.M.D.G.; nor with his holy medal; nor the length of his grace before meals.) But what was an essential fact was that, while revolted by any hint of philistinism in his form of belief, Thompson's imagination was permeated with the conviction that the personal embrace between Creator and creature was "solely the secret and note of Catholicism," and it was by this that his conduct was no less permeated. Patmore said of him: "He is of all men I have known most naturally a Catholic. My Catholicism was acquired, his inherent." An unknown critic in the *Athenaeum* wrote at his death: "What distinguishes him from the rest, at least among English poets—what gives him an impressiveness that has something Eastern in its quality—is that, when one arrives close enough to him, one finds him more than merely a poet. His claim is indeed threefold." After first designating him poet, then a man "who had sounded depths of misery deeper than most men," the writer continues: "he was, besides, not a saint, but a man who had the saint's intense, unfaltering preoccupation with eternal things, the saint's desire for God, whose passionate, individual apprehension of Christianity markedly affected that of his contemporaries."

Also on the side of his poor physique his life had been attuned not to indulgence but to asceticism.

This not unnatural judgment, in some of the obituary notices of Thompson, that he was an evil-doer if a remorseful one, was tempered by the allowance which had to be made for a poet. But such liberality was still only hurtful, and it was referring to it in an article in the *Dublin Review* that Alice Meynell wrote of Thompson's being the life of an elect soul, for which "no such condonation is called for." It was now that she spoke of many years of almost daily companionship having shown him to be "one of the most innocent of men."

The obituary note of a correspondent in *The Times* was the thing which prompted in Meynell a protest from which he could not keep out an emotional note. The correspondent had written: "There are occasions on which the conventional expression of regret becomes a mockery, and this is one of them. What the world must regret is not the release of Mr. Thompson, but the fact that the cravings of the body from which he is released should have power to ruin one of the most remarkable and original of the poetic geniuses of our time." Nothing was then known of the industry of Thompson's journalistic life—the mass of his literary criticism, anonymous in that day, which is since read as literature: and Meynell now in the *Nation* pointed out that Thompson's genius was not "ruined by the cravings of the body," but was abundantly used in his life and was ended by disease (he had only one lung, and that diseased, when he died). The idea that "regret was a mockery" Meynell countered with his own grief which made him "love his own life less because Thompson was dead."

There was another thing which Alice Meynell judged to be a misconception—this time the view that Thompson was "one of the unhappy poets." Everard Meynell also wrote of Thompson's life having "a superficial look of disaster and pain." But this opinion of two people singularly alive to others' suffering is impossible to accept now. There was disaster and pain in his life, there was also a seemingly wholehearted absorption in commonplaces. If at the time of his death, and when memory of all detail was still fresh, it was the trivial talk, the seeming abandonment of the whole man to trifling arrangements of, say, transport, or to a lost postage-stamp, or the merits of one tea-shop's buns over those of another—if these then seemed a fundamental mood in his life, they are the things which Time brings to the shallow surface, and the "superficial look of disaster and pain" becomes inherent. At the time of his death his somewhat girlish laugh could still be heard; his voice was still reiterating that his habit of stirring with his tea-spoon so violently that the contents of the cup spilled over was hereditary—for that kind of information was never given once and for all—and he was still explaining to his own satisfaction how punctual he would have been with his work but for some eccentricity of the clock. Thus Alice Meynell could consider that he had "natural good spirits," and she believed that "what darkness and oppression of spirit the poet underwent was over and past some fifteen years before he died," presumably referring to the period of his first struggle against opium. But it seems impossible that this opinion could have been held if there had been more time to survey fully such signs as were hidden in the partly indecipherable notebooks, phrases written for special moments but spreading their intimations forward and backward. "A most miserable fortnight of torpid despondent days & affrightful nights, dreams having been in part the worst realities of my life." Such an opinion, also, could have been held only in an age before complexities of feeling began to be taken into account, and when people were either happy or unhappy—never both. Now it even seems impossible to see in all the trivial commonplaces any alleviation from his unhappy life, for to his degree of sensibility all had the ominous significance of heavy Fate.

It is true that though few joys can be associated with a man who has no wife or family ties, so also are many griefs and anxieties spared him—and Thompson's existence was freer still than that, for he had none of the possessions which can give rise to uneasy guardianship and also to the desire for more. He was entirely without the impulse to own anything. (Spending much time at the Serendipity Shop, which certainly fulfilled its function of allurement, he occasionally took a detached interest in some object, but literary treasures as little suggested ownership to him as a landscape of hills and rivers would.) He died possessed of a few old pipes and old pens lying in a tin lid. He was also a property-owner of a casual collection of newspaper cuttings from the *Daily Mail*; the subjects he had saved were "Maria Blume's Will," "Insurance of Domestic Servants," "Help for the Householder," "Mikado Airs on Japanese Warship—Amusing Scenes"; "Freaks of Weather: Startling Changes of Temperature," "The Milk Peril, What Hinders Reform," and a poem by Sturge Moore.

When it is remembered how much else he did not collect of the things ordinarily prized—*i.e.* travel (he never crossed the Channel); and not only the landscapes and skies of a foreign land but even those of his own, for his eye was never on the look-out for visual impressions, and he was an alien in any country scene, not distinguishing between county characteristics nor knowing trees apart ("in a dungeon," Garvin had written, "he would be no less a poet")—when this is remembered and his degree of detachment becomes clearer, some link seems to develop between that and the smallness of his small-talk. Wilfrid Whitten's remark then seems a penetrating one: "On trifles he became grotesquely tedious: this dreamer seemed to be surprised into a kind of exhilaration at finding himself in contact with small realities." It is certain at any rate that he approached his trifling subjects with the curiosity of a stranger. A comment of almost startling aptness, on something of the same lines, was made by a writer in the *Athenaeum* in 1913. "The habit of his conversation, with its endless repetitions, excuses, explanations, and recounting of small matters, its heavy jokes and desolating platitudes, suggests some comparison with the disappointing triviality of utterances purporting to come from beyond the grave. It was, as it were, action that faltered across too great a distance."

An estimate of a man's level of contentment can hardly ignore his level of health, and Thompson's can rarely have allowed him anything but a low standard of comparative well or ill. On the other hand he was saved from some of the worst manifestations of his disease; he had, strangely, no cough and no haemorrhage.

But it was by poetry that his mind's condition was supremely governed. If it might easily be imagined that to be a poet is in itself to be liable to a greater susceptibility to suffering than the average, that was not Thompson's own view. "It is usual to suppose," he wrote, "that poets, because their feelings are more delicate than other men's, must needs suffer more terribly in the great calamities which agonise all men. But, omitting from the comparison the merely insensible, the idea may be questioned. The delicate nature stops at a certain degree of agony, as the delicate piano at a certain strength of touch." That the actual benefit lay with the poet was clear to him when he also wrote: "Deep grief or pain may find, and has in my case found, immediate outlet in poetry."

XIII

WILFRID MEYNELL was fifty-five at the time of Thompson's death. He was a home-stayer, as his journalism allowed him to be. For a time he was a member of the Savile Club but nothing suited him so well as home-life with a plentiful dash of restaurant-going; the Soho French restaurants were then the kind of club most to his taste, with his young family taken along as fellow members. He could not refrain from moving with a train of family, and one or two of them would be insinuated into the most desirable parties and private views, into artists' shows on "studio-Sunday," week-ends at Wilfrid Blunt's and dinners with him in London at Chapel Street. On some occasions, when the victimized hostess was not very well known to him, it was an operation which could have been conceived only by blind partiality and oblivion to convention.

As a journalist on many papers he was also able, as the children grew up, to sidle into the same papers their early attempts at journalism. He was an adept at paragraph-writing; it suited his episodic rather than historic mental picture. To the *Daily Chronicle's* two daily columns of miscellaneous paragraphs headed "From the Office Window" he despatched two or three every day; they were referred to by Alice Meynell in writing to him once as "your dear pathetic witty paragraphs"—pathetic because they were hard come by as an evening addition to the day's work; but at five shillings each it was a morning's amusement to see how many had got in, like looking for the result of a mild bet. And gradually some of the young members of the family got their paragraphs in too, and articles here and there, until at last he had occasion to write to one daughter of another: "The great thing now is to get a publisher for the book," and, having negotiated it, " I am all for Cape-ability publishing." He never turned down a journalistic commission, and as, in these pre-First-World-War days, papers had their ample social space, his adaptability led him to undertake such features as "Small Talk" or "Crowns, Coronets and Courtiers" for the weekly *Sketch*; but after starting off with exactly what was wanted, he would persuade a rather suspicious editor that his son could write the paragraphs equally well or better. Everard had married in 1910 the singer Grazia Carbone, and the livelihood he must now make was certainly sought by a diversity of means. His father helped him out with paragraphs when, as "Marigold" of the *Sketch*, Everard was too hard-pressed. The final smile of incongruity is supplied by the fact that Meynell was apt to work his convictions into the most unlikely surroundings, and Everard wrote to him once: "Thanks for your pars, but you had no sooner left than Goddard wrote to say that he thought there had been enough of Rome in the Socials. G. was quite nice. He said: 'Good as they are, per-haps there has been enough.'" Family letters at this time are full of the stress of journalism. "Everard hard at work till mid-night," his mother writes once. "I was able to do him a couple of feeble art pars. He was forcing an article on the Austrian Ambassador."

Meynell breathed publishing air; he had now only to go down three floors below the high flat and in an office there every morn-ing he dictated letters to the firm's secretary, Mr. Todd, and supervised the issuing of books not only written in the spirit of religion such as he rejoiced to disseminate, but in some cases affording the opportunity for the outstanding book production in which the firm now excelled. Meynell's interest in printing as one of the "little arts" had become a part of many of the things he did, and his influence on the style of book production was directly considerable, and indirectly vast. When he took charge of Burns and Oates, he entrusted to Bernard Newdigate the de-sign of its most important productions. Newdigate in 1903 had set out on his career as a fine printer by founding the Arden Press, and it was Meynell who gave him not merely his first important commission but the most favourable opportunity for noble bookmaking in the small folio "Of God and His Creatures,"[1] an annotated translation of the *Summa Contra Gentiles* of St. Thomas Aquinas by Joseph Rickaby, S.J. Meynell shared Newdigate's enthusiasm for Caslon Old Face, and used this type (and the services of Newdigate) for Thompson's Shelley essay, *Selected Poems* and the *Collected Works*. With his passion for detail, having discovered that a few stops at the ends of lines had broken off in the running off of the edition, Meynell had all the copies of the first printing of the *Collected Works*, in three volumes, delivered to his flat; and there a family chain was organized, one child opening the books, another handing them to Meynell who wrote in the stops, another using the blotting paper, another piling for the return to stock.

But besides drawing upon Newdigate in typographic matters, Meynell contrived that his youngest son Francis (whom he had put in charge of Burns and Oates' production) should have opportunities for learning the elements of typography from Newdigate; he encouraged Mr. Joseph Thorp in his propaganda at W. H. Smith's for better "printing for business"; and, most fortunate of all his typographic encouragements, he gave Mr. Stanley Morison employment, in both reviewing and book-designing, for an almost continuous period of some eight years, 1913 to 1921. Mr. Morison's memory of that period is expressed in a letter written after Wilfrid Meynell's death: "I have too abundant cause for gratitude not to remember W. M. until my own dying day."

Meynell's concern with typography had begun in early days when in 1887 Cardinal Manning made over to him the Westminster Press. Its works were in Harrow Road within a quarter of an hour of Palace Court—if walking broke into a run when proofs were urgent for the *Weekly Register*, which from 1888 was printed at the Westminster Press. In that year, according to the *Weekly Register*, "on the afternoon of Monday, June 11, Cardinal Manning visited the Westminster Press to inspect two new machines of which one was christened the 'Cardinal' and the

[1] It was chosen for the National Book League's Festival of Britain Exhibition of the 100 finest productions of the last fifty years.

other 'Lady Butler.'" On acquiring the press Meynell had taken into equal partnership his friend John George Snead-Cox, the editor of *The Tablet*. The fluctuating profits were small. One half-profit in one half-year, 1892, was £3 10s. 3½d.; in the next half-year each half-share was £81 19s. 11d. The press was eventually sold to Meynell's nephew Gerard Meynell in partnership with Claude Gibson.

Meynell had therefore at his command the means of producing in a manner after his own heart the works of Francis Thompson which a violent acceleration of interest following the poet's death demanded. As literary executor he could now devote his experience and judgment to editing and publishing. His first act was to send the forgotten Shelley essay, now rediscovered, to the *Dublin Review*, giving that quarterly the opportunity to redeem its original rejection of it under different editorship. When, eighteen years before, Meynell had seen the MS. of the essay and praised it, Thompson had written to him from Storrington: "Surprised about Shelley. Seemed to me dreadful trash when I read it over before sending it. Shut my eyes & ran to ye post, or some demon might have set me to work on picking it again." The effect of it now was sensational. The staid *Dublin* had the unique experience of leaping into a second edition; a leading article in the *Observer* was given to the "amazing literary event" of this "buried jewel" brought to light; and Thompson was now known as a prose writer. In the confusion of the notebooks also there were discoveries to be made: "In No Strange Land," the Shelley poem called "Buona Notte," and "Arab Love-Song."

The hunchèd camels of the night
Trouble the bright
And silver waters of the moon.
The Maiden of the Morn will soon
Through Heaven stray and sing,
Star gathering.

Now, while the dark about our loves is strewn,
Light of my dark, blood of my heart, O come!
And night will catch her breath up, and be dumb.

Leave thy father, leave thy mother
And thy brother;
Leave the black tents of thy tribe apart!
Am I not thy father and thy brother,
And thy mother?
And thou—what needest with thy tribe's black tents
Who hast the red pavilion of my heart?

A curious feature of Thompson's literary remains are his attempts at drama. A few short prose plays had been correctly and skilfully constructed, showing how much more spare enterprise his mind had than his body, for it is questionable if he ever entered a theatre. He had once written to Meynell: "I have summoned up pluck to send my little play [*Napoleon Judges: A Tragedy in Two Scenes*] (which Mrs. Meynell and you have seen) to William Archer, asking him whether it afforded any encouragement to serious study of writing for the stage. His answer is unfavourable—though he refrains from a precise negative. This sets my mind at rest on that matter. None the less, I wanted to read you one or two bits from my chucked-up *Saul*, since they seemed to be better than I knew." It appeared to Meynell now that William Archer's verdict could be rightly taken to cover the various attempts, and they remained unpublished.

In the meantime Meynell had been preparing *Selected Poems*, and it appeared in the year following Thompson's death, 1908. The result was again completely unexpected by former standards; the book started on a career of unending sales. An entry in Blunt's *Diaries* in 1910 is: "Meynell tells me the sale of Thompson's works during the past 12 months has gone to 18,000 volumes." In 1909 Burns and Oates also published, for a more limited public, *St. Ignatius Loyola*, which was complete when Thompson died. Then in 1913 appeared *The Works of Francis Thompson* in three volumes, one of them prose. It was the bringing into existence of the complete counterpart of the man, the body of his mind made whole and perfect. Meynell wrote to an American friend in this year: "I have had a surprise in the extraordinary public interest.

Having known the Poet during 20 years of obscurity, I cannot get accustomed to the new order of things."

The question had arisen soon after Thompson's death of the need of a Life. Meynell had never thought he had himself any real claim to being a writer; he had been too closely connected with considerable writers not to know that his had been a more jobbing rôle, and that any glow of authorship he might sometimes feel was a rather more private than public concern. He had, besides, the prevailing instinct to provide his family with opportunities to make their own way, and in the case of Everard a conviction that he had outstanding gifts to be used. Everard had already written a monograph on Giovanni Bellini, and *Corot and His Friends*. His relationship with Thompson had been singularly close—affectionate, understanding, admiring. He was given the task, and the *Life* appeared in the same year as the *Collected Works*. Both were Burns and Oates publications. To Meynell his wife had written in his absence, and before he had himself seen the proofs of the book, "I am sure you will be very much impressed by his digest of F. T.'s philosophy and theology. It is excellent. He and I together have pruned the rather strange phrases that sounded too much searched for." And later: "It is indeed beautiful writing, of which anyone might be proud." This *Life*, with its chapters on "Words, Origins and Metres," and on "Mysticism and Imagination," and with its remarkable all-round grasp of his subject, showed the connoisseurship and wide reading of its author, who was still in his twenties when he was writing it. Some years later he pruned it still further of the somewhat elaborate essay-style which had appealed to him earlier.

It had already happened, in 1911, that the narrow London quarters were supplemented by a country-dwelling for the Meynells, when a small seventeenth-century house with eighty acres of common and woodland was bought, at no more than £20 an acre, in Sussex under the South Downs, a few miles from Storrington where Thompson had first begun to find his power as a poet. This was another of Meynell's plunges, and long continued to seem a good-fortune fairy tale. The house was at

ALICE MEYNELL

in late life

WILFRID MEYNELL
Portrait by Olivia Sowerby in 1936

Greatham, a place remotely situated, without a village; and if the question were asked what it was near it was only possible to name the nearest place it was far from. There was now constant coming and going, and if the whole idea had originated in the wish to give the walking-touring young family more country life, by the time Meynell had planned and directed operations there, his remarkable ingenuity coming into play, no one more revelled in the possession than he himself. His development of it made it specially his own, as Alice Meynell recognized when she called it "your Greatham." "Your Greatham is looking heavenly," she wrote to him. "May it all be a joy to you, my own dearest." From now on, Greatham information was bandied about in the family. Meynell wrote to a grandchild:

We went to a sale at the Pulborough Repository yesterday & bought:

3 wooden chairs	10/–
1 iron bedstead	9/–
1 small chest of drawers	£1 15
1 box	8/–
1 lawn mower	5/–

The latter was knocked down to me without my bidding. I just happened to catch the eye of Newland Tompkins. But as it is a great bargain, I don't grumble. It is only 10 inches wide & it has no box. But it cuts beautifully & does not fatigue the driver. There was a lot of rain in the night. It blew the vine down, beheaded the roses, & beat up the earth till the strawberries became strawburys.

It was in a library added to the small house that he now read poetry aloud to visiting friends, and he was inclined to think an occasion became a little frivolous unless redeemed by some acknowledgment of the world of poetry. "How much of a poetry reader are you: are you a sufficient Thompsonian?" That was what he wanted to know of people near and far, and to-day's answer to the latter part was different from the blank he drew before Thompson's death. All testimonies were welcome to him, to tell again. The *Life of Burne-Jones* had revealed how, though the operation of dressing and undressing was one that he loathed, after first reading "The Hound of Heaven" Burne Jones was so oblivious to everything that he forgot that he was undressing, and dressed instead, and had to undress again. Meredith had called Thompson "a true poet, one of the small band." The other novelist-and-poet might have had a further road to travel to the profuse Thompson, but Hardy wrote in 1913: "You may be sure I am a Thompsonian 'sufficient' enough to accept with great pleasure the very kind present of his works. If I can deserve it by appreciating Thompson more than I have hitherto done I shall be glad indeed, but it will be difficult, for, as you probably know, I have already set no small value on him as a poet, packed as full of jewels as Keats." In an undated letter to Blunt, Meynell wrote: "A great thing as you say is the success of the books. Thompson can now be left to take care of himself. About 20,000 volumes of the Collected Works have been sold, & on Xmas day the Dean of Westminster proclaimed his name from the pulpit in Westminster Abbey—a mention which is nearly as good as a tablet on its walls, though that must somehow or other be brought about."

Greatham had not long been fully organized when visits to it became doubly welcome in the strain of wartime. The distress of war was overwhelming to one of Alice Meynell's unsparing imagination; her only relief, like that of other mothers, was when by family-assembly there could be a momentary illusion of love prevailing; and the now-scattered family got there sometimes. (They had been at Greatham when war was declared; and at the tiny church at Houghton, when the death of Pope Pius X occurred, heard from the young priest in the pulpit the effective phrase: "The nations of the world have declared war upon each other, and God has withdrawn His ambassador.")

For Meynell there was now the outlet of his leap into tractarian popularity with *Aunt Sarah and the War* and its successors. The most-read weekly of that time, *Land and Water*, in which Belloc made his famous military commentaries, had another feature in the form of a page "By the Author of Aunt Sarah and the War." He balanced other people's "letters to lonely soldiers" by heading his page "Letters to a Lonely Civilian." As in *Aunt Sarah*, he spilled his mind of its miscellaneous store of anecdote and reference without being at much pains to make a coherent sequence, except in so far as all went the way of his own convictions. But a general tone of toleration and broad-mindedness was always present in what he wrote in spite of his ardent beliefs; and the inevitable touch of sentiment (the Letters began: "My dear You") did not lessen the appeal of all this writing. During the war he also acted as deputy editor of the *Dublin Review*. He had reached his early sixties. Such editorial functions now went back into a distant perspective. "I have been refusing an article against Protestants by Sir Henry Bellingham," he mentioned in writing to a daughter, "and I think it must be the same article that I refused in the same terms 20 years ago for *Merry England*."

The traffic between Greatham and the flat in Granville Place was kept up, as the winters indicated one place and the summers the other. The Greatham house was unheated except by log-fires and unlit except by candles. A recurring incident was the reduced family arriving from Greatham at the high flat in London on some bitter day. Down in a studio in Burns and Oates, Meynell had installed two Austrian peasant-craftsmen to carve wooden figures as an improvement on normal church statuary, and he would send down for a sack of the wood-shavings with which their floor was littered, and with these start a heartening blaze. And another recurring incident was the descent in the night into the Burns and Oates bookish and statued cellars until an all-clear sounded. It was a time when distraction was invaluable. "We have just read a course of O. Henry," he wrote to an American friend in 1917. "Read him at once if you haven't already. He has just the needed knack of the short story; & though there's no damned literature about him even Alice falls at his feet. He is direct without brutality, slangy without malignity, & has such nobility of view that if you ever differ from him you know you're a devil, so there! It seems that he went to prison for taking something not his own,[1] & I not there to make good!—two lapses for which his patron saint and mine must render strict account at the Last Judgment." On Easter Sunday, 1917, he wrote to the same friend: "I can't keep quiet. America & England united States!—always so, in love, with me, but now at last in official fact."

With the end of the war, and in the peace which for so long was still painful with it, years of comparative leisure began for Meynell. As he approached the age of seventy he was, in energy and decision, very much the middle-aged man. "We both feel very old," he wrote however to a friend in 1921, "and though Alice's hair refuses to grey I have hardly even a white one left." With the zest of a young collector he occasionally bought books and autographs. He dwelt a good deal on the hobby-side of the love of literature, liking to stow and show things of interest at Greatham, making a Sussex collection there, concentrating association books and autographs and the treasures he had acquired over a long period by dint of being both shrewd and reckless. Long ago Lord Leighton's possessions, sold after his death, had been the occasion of the acquisition of good Persian rugs and a fine collection of architectural photographs. In 1912, the sale of the Brownings' effects when Mrs. Pen Browning died had yielded things of unique interest (among them the only letter written by Browning to his wife, from whom he was never apart, after their marriage, and a photograph of herself given by her to him "with all my love and very little likeness"). The most conspicuous treasure from that source, housed in a niche in the Greatham library, was a bust of Shelley, acquired by the rare accidental luck of the sale-room in this wise (the purest piece of serendipity): Meynell had once visited at his studio the engraver William Bell Scott and seen there his engraving of Mrs. Leigh Hunt's bust of Shelley. Having made the engraving William Bell Scott had

[1] The *Everyman Encyclopaedia* says: "Fate seemed to have dealt him a finishing blow when, in 1896, he was arrested on the charge of embezzling some of the funds of the Austin bank. The episode was never entirely cleared up. What is known is that in 1898 he was sentenced to five years' imprisonment in the Ohio Penitentiary. This was reduced to three years by good behaviour."

affixed to it his monogram, **W. B. S.** At the Browning sale, the only known cast of the bust, which had been in Browning's possession, was included, but the maker of the catalogue, knowing nothing of it, and seeing a copy of the engraving, had decided that the monogram should be interpreted as **W. S. B.**, *i.e.* William Shergold Browning, and that the bust must therefore be the portrait of Browning's uncle of that name. When the lot came up, Meynell recognized it and rose to his feet to inform the auctioneer that it was the bust of Shelley, but he replied that it would be sold as catalogued, and Meynell was able to buy for the sum of £13 the only known copy of the only realistic likeness —though made posthumously—of Shelley (Miss Curran's prevailing pretty portrait being, as she herself knew, "so ill done.")

Among the manuscripts in the Greatham library were Coventry Patmore's *Angel in the House* and the complete *Odes*, given by him to Alice Meynell.

Into the abundant Thompson manuscripts and letters Meynell was often delving to bestow something on any stranger who was a "sufficient Thompsonian."

But what formed the very essence of the library, speaking more than all else of unending interest and devotion, was the collection of everything that concerned Alice Meynell's work. Since the day long ago when he had first seen a sonnet in a paper, and as an unformed young man had known that the mere relation of writer and reader must somehow be surpassed, Meynell had preserved the same intimate delight in her writing. Illumined by personal reasons and agreements, her poetry had as much of his love as Francis Thompson's—but for one thing: in its method of expression it was restrained, it practised a severe economy of words, preoccupied with sense and not sound. For this reason her early, more fluent poems were preferred by him to her later ones; and this was a division of opinion between them which compelled her to do violence to her own predilections. (For in the arrangement of her volumes and editions, which came under his expert hand, he gave precedence to the earlier poems which she would have liked suppressed or made inconspicuous. His skill in print-ing-publishing details had given him so much natural ascendancy that he was tempted to extend its province.) But if he preferred those poems of hers which flowed most musically, he needed to use no such discrimination in regard to Thompson, in whom sheer sound was always abundantly present or predominant. Musically, Meynell was tone-deaf; it would be interesting to know if those who are tone-deaf are the more likely to take out their sympho-nies and concertos in that poetry which is the most soundful.

In the late summer of 1922 Wilfrid Meynell went abroad. He wrote to Blunt:

7 Casa Petrarca, Venice. 3 Sept. 1922.

My dear Blunt,

When you see this address you will see that I have taken temporary leave of my country—& my senses. But Viola & Olivia insisted on bringing me to outlandish parts, & we are here on our way to Ragusa in Dalmatia, a three days' sail down the Adriatic. I did not mean to go abroad again, but I am not sorry to be reminded of the beauty of Italy which, all the way from Milan to here, exceeds one's absent thoughts of it. And the vitality of the Venetians! Babies walk out by themselves, & every small boy is a bravo. The many women who look like young Disraelis bring back his own story of the expulsion of his ancestors from Spain & their settlement here. Very beautiful they are, of the Madonna type which their Jewish blood flatters and confirms. I have often wished you could tell me this, that, & the other thing that arises in the mind questioningly in this most cosmopolitan place, & among the most cosmo-politan people known to my narrow experience. I look forward to Newbuildings at the end of the month.

Yours affectionately,
Wilfrid Meynell

With the young family all married or marrying, and grand-children beginning to populate Greatham as a foretaste of the way in which it was to become a patriarchal home, Meynell was no longer scribbling for dear life—though nothing could part him from his pencil-and-paper preoccupation with neatly turned verses and quick word-play; and when a grandchild was born who was named Catherine it was the work of a minute to turn her into an anagram:

> So many, dearest, fail of pace,
> But you are always *in the race*.

In these easier times his grandchildren knew a more carefree man than the hard-driven companion he had been to his children. Where those had seen him spinning out the words of his livelihood, the new generation was accustomed to idler words. Of consideration and helpfulness towards his family there was no diminution as all by degrees embarked on their own independent efforts.

But he had one first interest in life. Alice Meynell had always so unemphasized her hard-working fragility that care of her had been enforced in the face of her own ignoring of it. It was not physical courage or aid that she ever wanted; what she valued was the moral strength that came with Meynell into a room, as it had come in wartime and in all mental stresses. But in these postwar years the need for cherishing her strength had become more obvious and more yielded to. It was not that she seemed old. John Drinkwater's was the impression that she gave universally: "I have never known anyone so ageless. Youth, maturity and fulness of years were here strangely at one." And she had lately written some of her best poems. The thought of death was not consistent with such timeless spirit and powers. But in the winter of 1922 she became gravely weak and ill. She died on November 27.

XIV

MEYNELL was not the kind of man to recover from his loss. He had much happiness coming—his love of the natural objects seen at Greatham, the clouds and trees, amounting to a kind of ecstasy. He had exceedingly valued friendships; Sir Shane Leslie was one with whom he carried on the tradition of affinity with the individualist (his visits were so common that his wife would say "he's Meynelling"). And in Meynell's latest years a young man of uncommon gifts of mind and heart, Father Gervase Mathew, was his devoted friend and confessor. He had also as the years went by the pleasure of welcoming great-grandchildren as they were added to the throng visiting Greatham. He was besides relieved of all pressure of work. What had made the change in his fortunes? —the change from the crisis of the unexpected bill and the extra article to be written to meet it, to a condition of modest affluence? First, his surprising success as a man of business in conducting the publishing house of Burns and Oates, which had paid him a modest salary but substantial dividends on the shares which the other two proprietors, Riddel Blunt and J. G. Snead-Cox, had made available to him. Secondly, royalties on his own books, *Aunt Sarah and the War* and its successor, were surprisingly large. Alice Meynell's works also sold after her death in far larger numbers than during her life. And finally Francis Thompson's poems sold as many hundreds after his death as they had sold units while he was alive—a recompense to Meynell, who was left Thompson's literary property, of poetic justice.

But though he could and did congratulate himself on many things, he was of the kind that is stricken with fundamental loneliness without the all-important primacy in love which has hitherto been possessed. The long remainder of his life was lived in the need of her who had, he said, "fulfilled for me Crashaw's 'heaven on earth' for forty-five years."

There was another loss. Everard Meynell, held by his family to be a man of rare perception, judgment, and courage, died at the beginning of 1926, from lung-trouble dating from his service in the Artists' Rifles.

In the nineteen-thirties and 'forties Meynell was endlessly pleased by the existence of a Francis Thompson Museum at the library of Boston College, started by the zeal of the Jesuit Father Terence Connolly, who devoted years of research to identifying the mass of Thompson's anonymous writing, and unearthed much high-level prose. In this old age of his, any word Meynell heard concerning either of his two poets was the best word he could hear; such transatlantic specialized love of Thompson, therefore, in which Father Connolly with charm and grace made him feel he was integrally included, brought him much consciousness of triumph. So did the constant signs he received of Thompson's influence. "How almost miraculous is the effect which one poem, *The Hound of Heaven*, is having on the revival of religious feeling in England," he wrote to Father Connolly. To him too he wrote in 1938 as the world grew darker with the threat of war: "Saturday is to be the day of deadly settlement or of the almost equally horrible continuance of national hatreds." But when the years of war came, he had begun to enter into the detachment of extreme old age; he could not, or did not, follow its course; the fact was enough. To involve the whole of his feeling some close personal incident was needed. A bomb fell on November 5, 1944, in a field adjoining the Greatham property. He was away, but the cottage he had built for a daughter was blasted.

> You will know what sympathy goes to you from all here [he wrote]—from me perhaps more than all, for as the house's owner I feel in some way especially responsible for what you have suffered, & for what you *might have* suffered, too terrible to imagine without agony. Words fail me to tell you all I feel, but my gratitude goes to Heaven for your escape. My

thoughts are with you all day long. The speedy help that has come is a great comfort to me. And please, if there are expenses, pay freely on my account, letting me know my indebtedness.

When he stayed in London it was at 47 Palace Court which he re-occupied after letting it for more than twenty years, sharing it with members of his family. His contacts, as ever, included beggars on the streets. Mere almsgiving was too humourless, too inhuman. He held his hands behind his back and made it a matter of guessing in which hand was a half-crown, and in which a penny. Besides getting his half-crown, the recipient, who always guessed right, had the almost incredulous enjoyment of good luck in a fair and square game—enhanced by Meynell's dramatic air of being the loser.

During these London visits he went to Sir John Lavery's studio in South Kensington to sit for his portrait. On these and other occasions taxis were used, and Meynell had a habit, after getting stiffly out of the cab, of saying to the driver as he paid him: "Take my advice: never be ninety; it isn't worth it." After a moment's surprise the response was always one of singularly smiling understanding and appreciation, and a friend was made. The old woman awaiting alms on her stool outside church each Sunday was his "sweetheart," and her own joke to him was that she was "Waiting at the church!"

It was in the 'forties that he was in his ninth decade; he looked twenty years younger. He depended much on old age's mild amusements—not for a long time past even going to see a film, for he had to report that "the last time they took me to a film, long ago, I fell asleep, justifying Shelley's allusion to 'gentle sleep, the filmy-eyed.' " It was rather his evening game of word-making, called "lexicon," played by the fireside, that came easily to his familiar turn of mind; and as he made it easier still by abstracting the difficult letters from the alphabet-pack, the j and x and z, he again indulged his turn of mind by calling it "laxicon." Or in the Greatham garden in the sun he worked at The Times crossword with some companion, and perhaps when some item of knowledge was required which he had never possessed, his old-age bad memory played him the flattering trick of allowing him to think he had only forgotten it.

In 1943 he was made a C.B.E., a thing which surprised and pleased him in the empty days of old age.

He wandered round the bookshelves lining the library walls, able to choose out long-read books to read as new. His spirit must haunt that room as a gardener his garden. It happened several times that his friend Father Ignatius Rice came from Douai and set up an altar against the bookshelves and said Mass for him there; and, as in lieu of holy pictures the Sargent drawing of Alice Meynell and Everard's drawing of Francis Thompson happened to hang near, for Meynell it must have been like a Mass said in the presence of his saints.

There was nothing particularly valiant about his endurance of the discomforts of this extreme old age; they made another claim for the companionship and love which were his great need, and as such they were not played down. As other things in life became remote, the love which was what religion meant to him he needed to feel in every contact of every day. It is told of Dr. John Brown's grandfather (John Brown of Whitburn) that he kissed first his grandson and then his grandson's rabbits. If so he was a fellow spirit. In Meynell's tenderness for all life, his thankfulness for any human presence, reluctance when the footsteps went another way, his words of endearment which were half the words he said, there was a thinning-out of his existence to one thing —the fondness that was also a prayer for fondness.

He reached the age of ninety-six, and died in October, 1948, and was buried at Storrington.

He had never made any claims for himself, being thankful for no achievement so much as for his mere bread-winning one. The fame he had desired was for others. But through his many years he had been a man of the enlightened liberal views which any age is in need of, and by means of his industrious journalism this influence travelled far and long. His self-written epitaph gives his own summing-up.

When my last fires of life burn low
(I who had loved all fire-light so),
When hence you bear my load of dust
To the grave's pit as bear you must,
Remember that naught perisheth
In all God's universe but Death.
Weep not, though tears be holy water,
Tears of a wife, a son, a daughter.
Think of me only when you laugh;
And if you write my epitaph,
No name or date be there, but rather
Here lies Her Husband and Their Father.

To the few who knew one of the subjects of this brief account, and the many who knew the other, each seemed to be among the most lovable of men.

INDEX

Academy, The, 41, 85, 121, 123, 140
Ackworth School, Croydon, 2
Alma-Tadema, Sir Laurence, 24
Alphonsus, Fr., 40
Anselm, Fr. (Archbishop of Simla), 40–41, 52, 107
Archer, William, 127, 195
Arden Press, 192
Arnold, Sir Edwin, 110
Arnold, Matthew, 7, 51
Art Journal, The, 24, 140
Ashton-under-Lyme, 13, 14, 55–6
A Sister's Story, 2
Athenæum, The, 85, 123, 135, 140, 151, 181, 186
Aunt Sarah and the War, 198, 204
Austin, Alfred, 7, 102, 110, 185

Belloc, Hilaire, 10, 20, 82
Bennett, Arnold, 54
Blackburn, Mrs., 29, 51–2
Blunt, E. Riddel, 204
Blunt, Wilfrid Scawen, 10, 23, 74–85, 147, 178–9, 181, 185, 191, 195, 202
Bookman, The, 55, 103
Bootham School, 1–2
Bournemouth, 60, 62
Bridges, Robert, 51
Brien, Maggie, 93
Browning, E. B., 146
Browning, Robert, 7, 38–9, 87, 102, 200–1
Bunyan, 160
Burnand, Sir Francis, 149
Burne-Jones, 198
Burns & Oates, 7 *n.*, 10, 130, 133, 135, 141, 178, 192–3, 195, 204
Butler, Lady (Elizabeth Thompson), 7, 11, 46, 194
Butler, Sir William, 11, 75, 144
Byron, 142

Capuchins, The, 40, 77–8

Carbone, Grazia (Mrs. Everard Meynell), 179, 181–2, 192
Chambers, E. K., 54
Chatterton, 23
Chesterton, 161
Cockerell, Sir Sydney, 80
Coleridge, 34, 176
Compton, Herbert, 3
Connolly, Fr. Terence, S.J., 205
Cowley, 105
Crabbet Park, Sussex, 78–9
Crashaw, 103, 105, 205
Craven, Mrs., 2
Crawhall, Joseph, 138
Crawley, 29 *n.*, 40–2, 173–5
Cuthbert, Fr., 40, 77–8

Daily Chronicle, The, 92, 135, 140, 150 191
Davidson, John, 50
Davies, W. H., 16–17
De Quincey, 14, 20, 34
De Vere, Aubrey, 10, 43, 58–9
Disraeli, 130, 141, 147, 149–50, 202
Dobson, Austin, 7
Doubleday, Mr. and Mrs. Arthur, 117
Dreyfus, 143
Drinkwater, John, 203
Dublin Review, The, 31, 33, 83, 141–2, 187, 194, 199
Dumas, 123

Edinburgh Review, The, 56
Ely Place, St. Etheldreda's, 4, 9, 59

Fortnightly Review, The, 74, 105
Franciscan Annals, 41
Frey, L., 116
Friston, 119, 166

Garibaldi, 146
Garvin, J. L., 50, 55, 99–102, 189
George, Henry, 65–6

209

Gibson, Claude, 194
Gladstone, 141–2
Gordon, 64
Greatham, 196, 198–9, 205
Quincy, Louise Imogen, 39

Hamilton, Lord George, 149
Hamilton, Sir William Rowan, 62
Hardy, Thomas, 198
Henley, W. E., 35, 51, 123
Henry, O., 199–200
Hind, C. L., 121, 123, 140
Hood, Thomas, 151
Housman, A. E., 80
Housman, Laurence, 46
Hudson, W. H., 10
Hunt, Mrs. Leigh, 200

Ignatius Loyola, St., 170, 178, 195
Illustrated London News, The, 135, 140
Inkerman Terrace, 9

Jacobs, W. W., 182
Johnson, Doctor, 10
Johnson, Lionel, 10, 39–40

Keats, 34, 82, 128, 198
King, Mrs. Hamilton, 93, 95–7, 144–6
King, Katharine Douglas (Mrs. Godfrey
    Burr), 93–9

Lamp, The, 5, 7
Land and Water, 198
Lane, John, 43, 56, 101
Lavery, Sir John, 206
Lawrence, Miss, 180
Leadenhalle Presse, 138
Le Gallienne, R., 51
Leslie, Lady, 149
Leslie, Sir Shane, 204
Lockhart, Fr. William, Inst.Ch., 4–9,
    59, 67
Lucas, Winifred (Mrs. Le Bailly), 94
Lucy, Sir Henry, 141
Lymington, 107, 112–13
Lyttelton, Alfred, 142
Lytton, Neville, 179

Macaulay, 160
Manchester, 14–15
Manchester Guardian, The, 102

Manning, Cardinal, 4, 9, 65, 67, 150,
    193
Marianus, Fr., 42
Martin Chuzzlewit, 180
Massingham, W. H., 123
Mathew, Fr. Gervase, O.P., 204
MacCarthy, Sir Desmond, 80
McMaster, Mrs., 18–20
Meredith, George, 40, 85, 95, 106, 137,
    141, 146
Mercure de France, 185
Merry England, 10–12, 22, 28–9, 36–7,
    94, 101, 199,
Meynell, Alice, 5–9, 35–6, 41, 43–6,
    48, 51–2, 55–9, 63–4, 71–3, 79, 85,
    87–92, 106–7, 110, 117, 129, 131,
    135–6, 138, 151, 183, 188, 191, 196–7,
    203
Meynell, Everard, 129, 178, 181–2,
    188, 192, 196, 205, 207
Meynell, Sir Francis, 119, 193
Meynell, Gerard Tuke, 194
Meynell, Madeline (Mrs. Lucas), 53
Meynell, Monica (Mrs. Saleeby), 53,
    93, 118, 120, 129, 137, 166, 172
Meynell, Philip, 3
Meynell, Samuel Tuke, 84, 148
MEYNELL, WILFRID, birth and parent-
    age, 1; schooling, 2; joins Roman
    Catholic Church, 2, 134; embarks
    on journalism, 3; Verses by Three
    Friends, 3; friendship with Father
    Lockhart, and residence at St.
    Etheldreda's, Ely Place, 4; engage-
    ment and marriage, 6–9; Inkerman
    Terrace, 9; The Pen, a Journal of
    Literature, 9; friendship with Aubrey
    de Vere, 58–61; and Sir Henry
    Taylor, 60–4; Journals and Journalism,
    62–3, 138; The Cousins, 140; friend-
    ship with Manning, 9, 65–8; edits
    The Weekly Register, 9, 146, 193;
    Upper Phillimore Place, 11; Merry
    England produced and edited, 10–12;
    meeting with Francis Thompson,
    24–7; house at Palace Court, 24, 35,
    117; Faith Found in London, 149–50;
    friendship with Mivart, 69–71, 74;
    connection with Burns and Oates, 130,
    171, 192–3, 199; contributions to
    various journals, 24, 139–44, 192,
    198; earnings, 135–6, 141, 204;